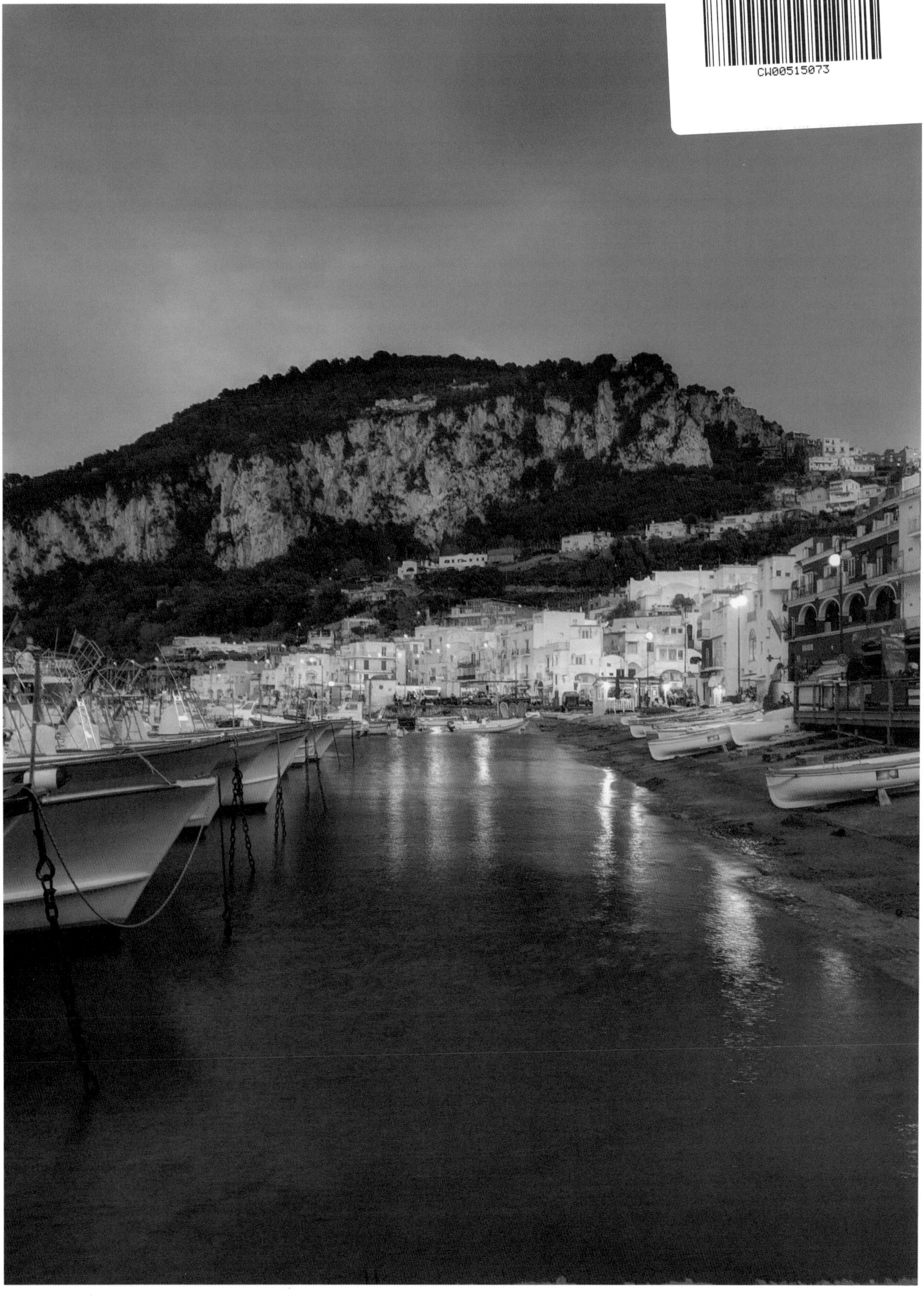

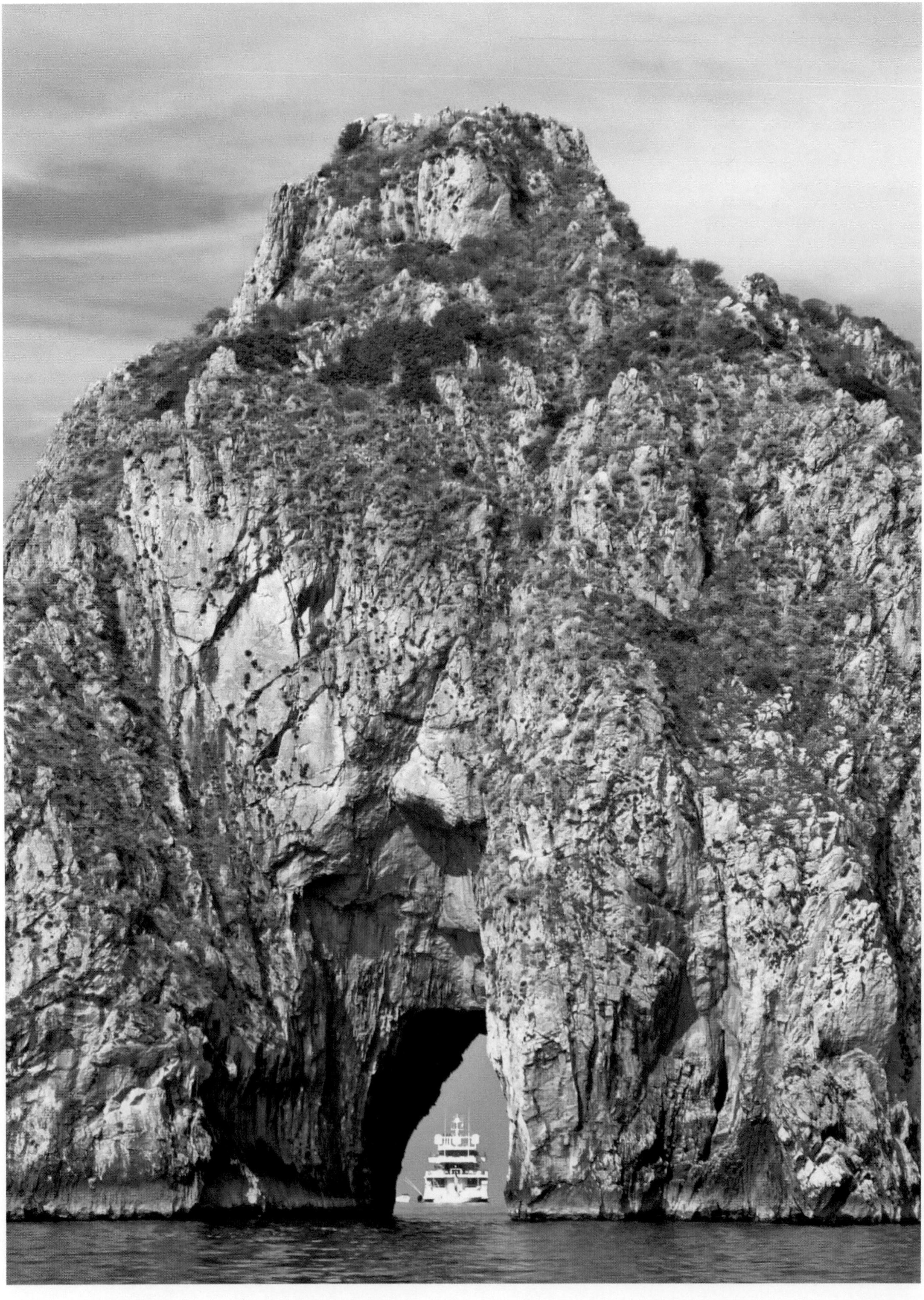

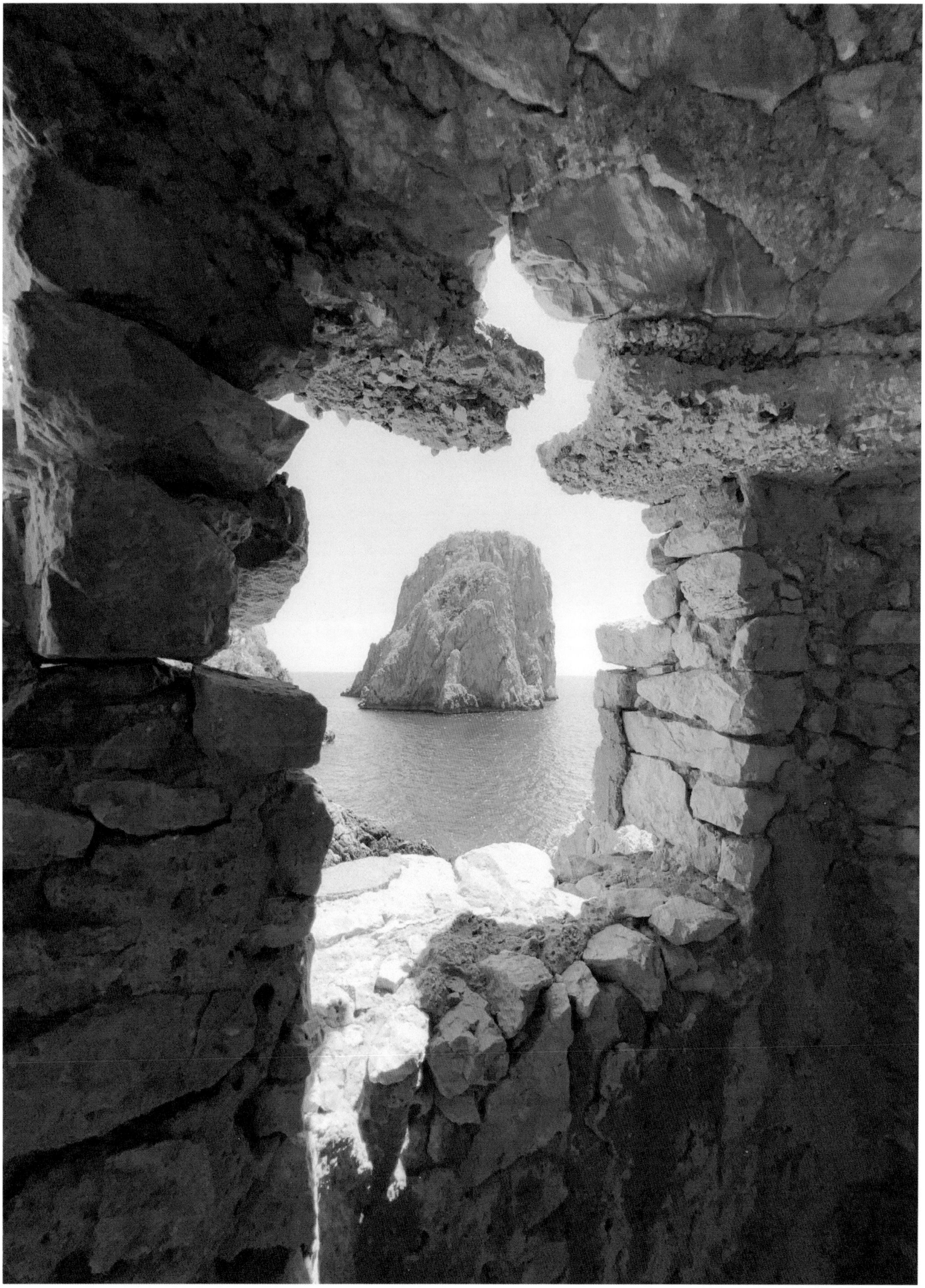

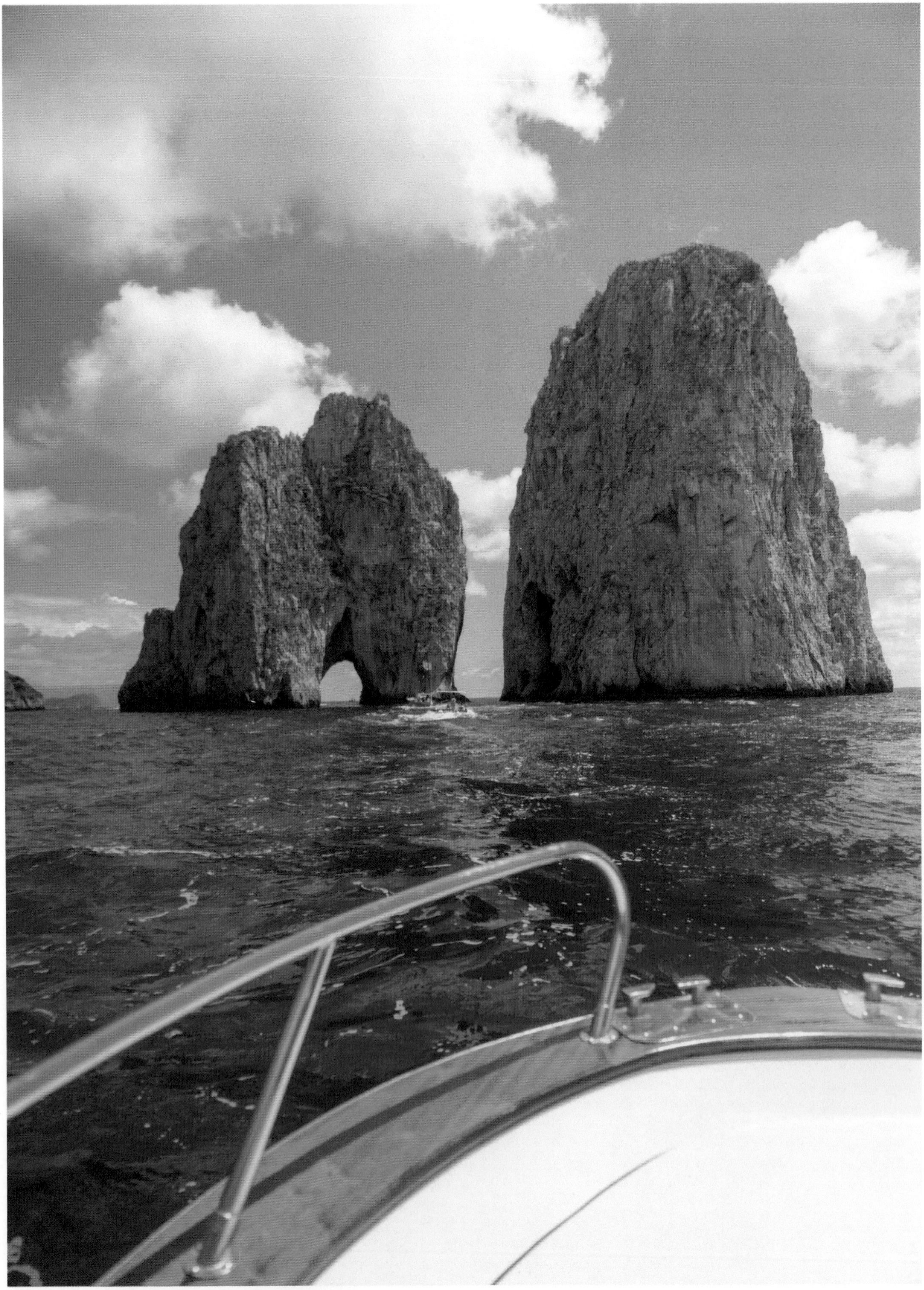

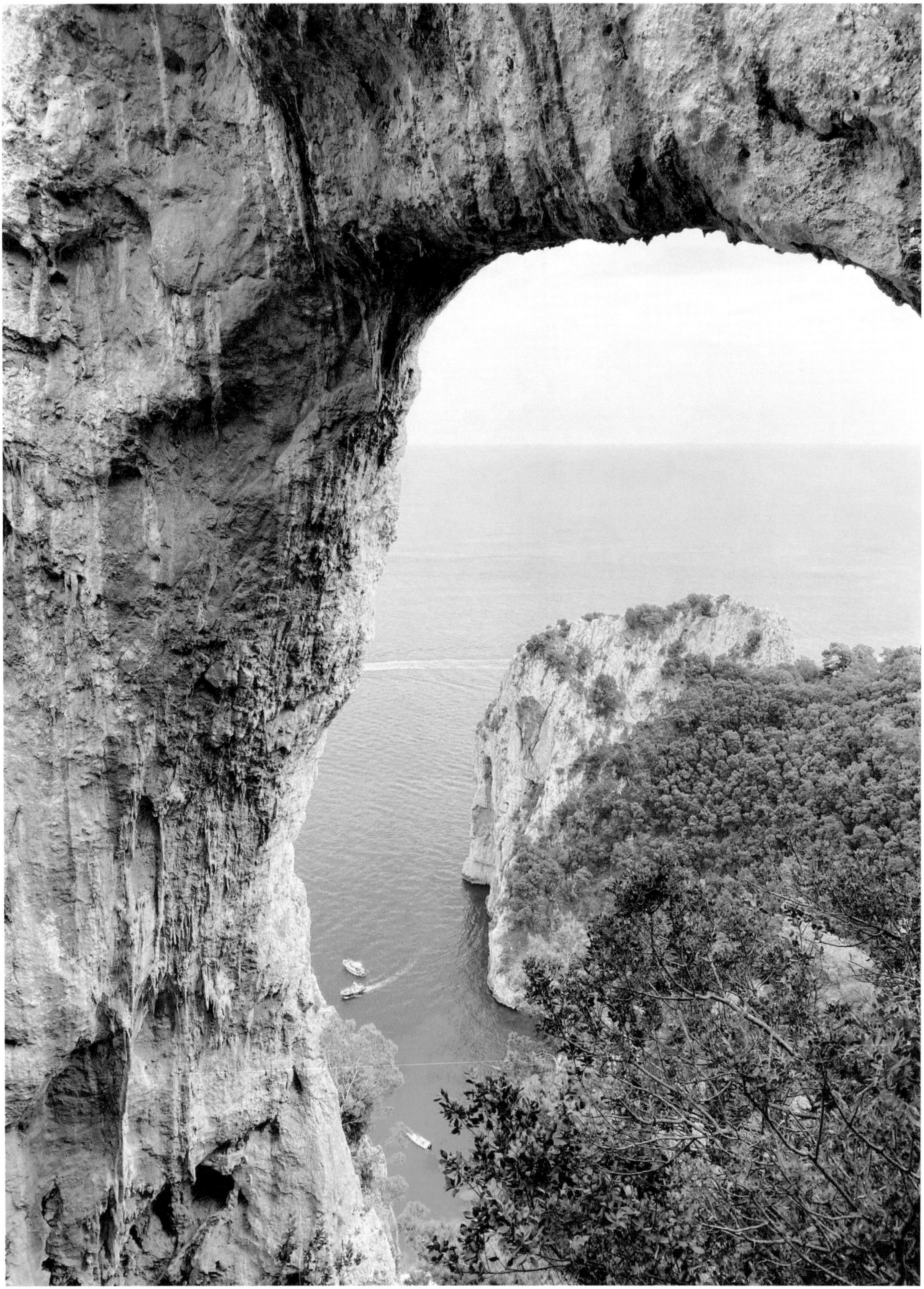

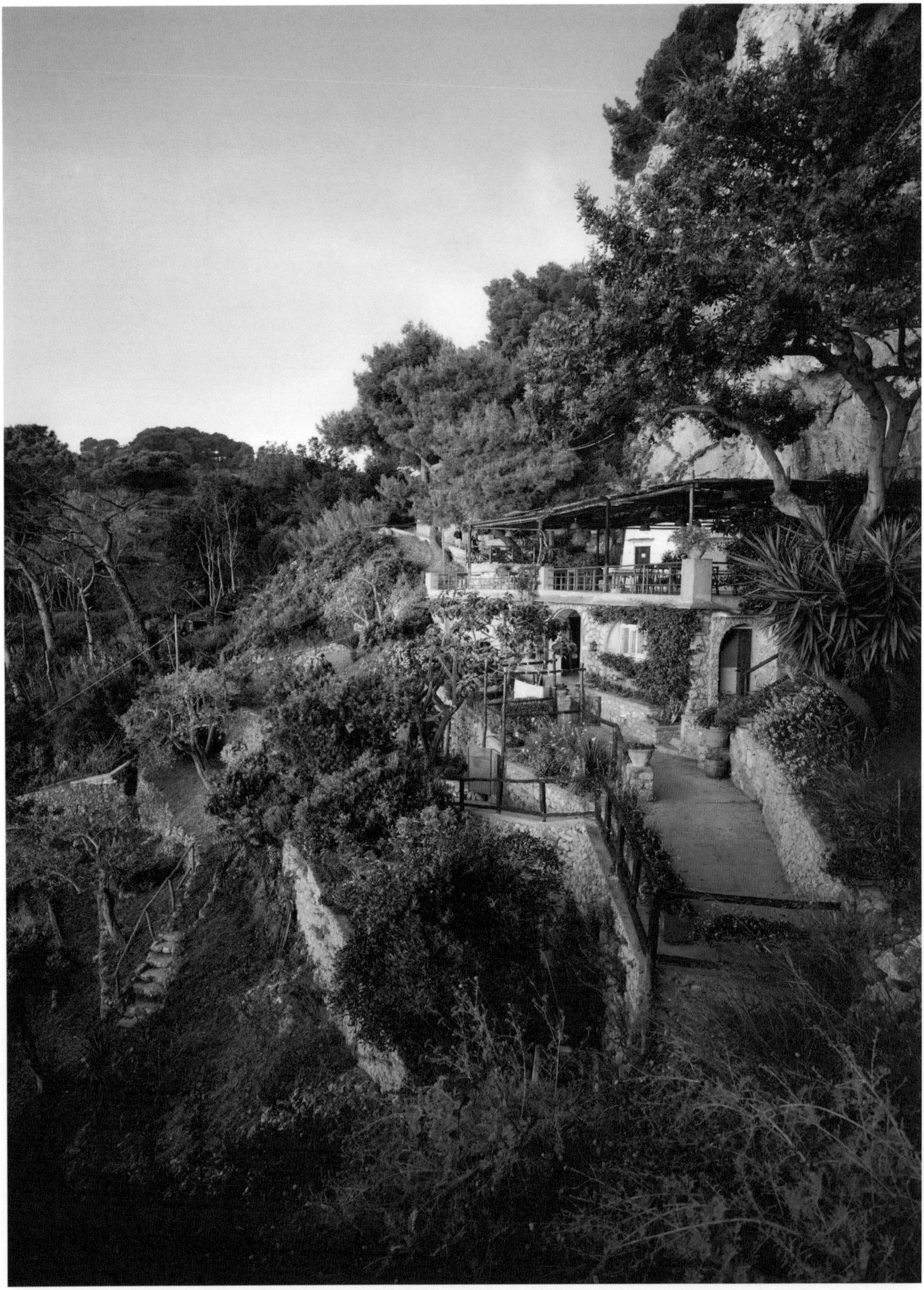

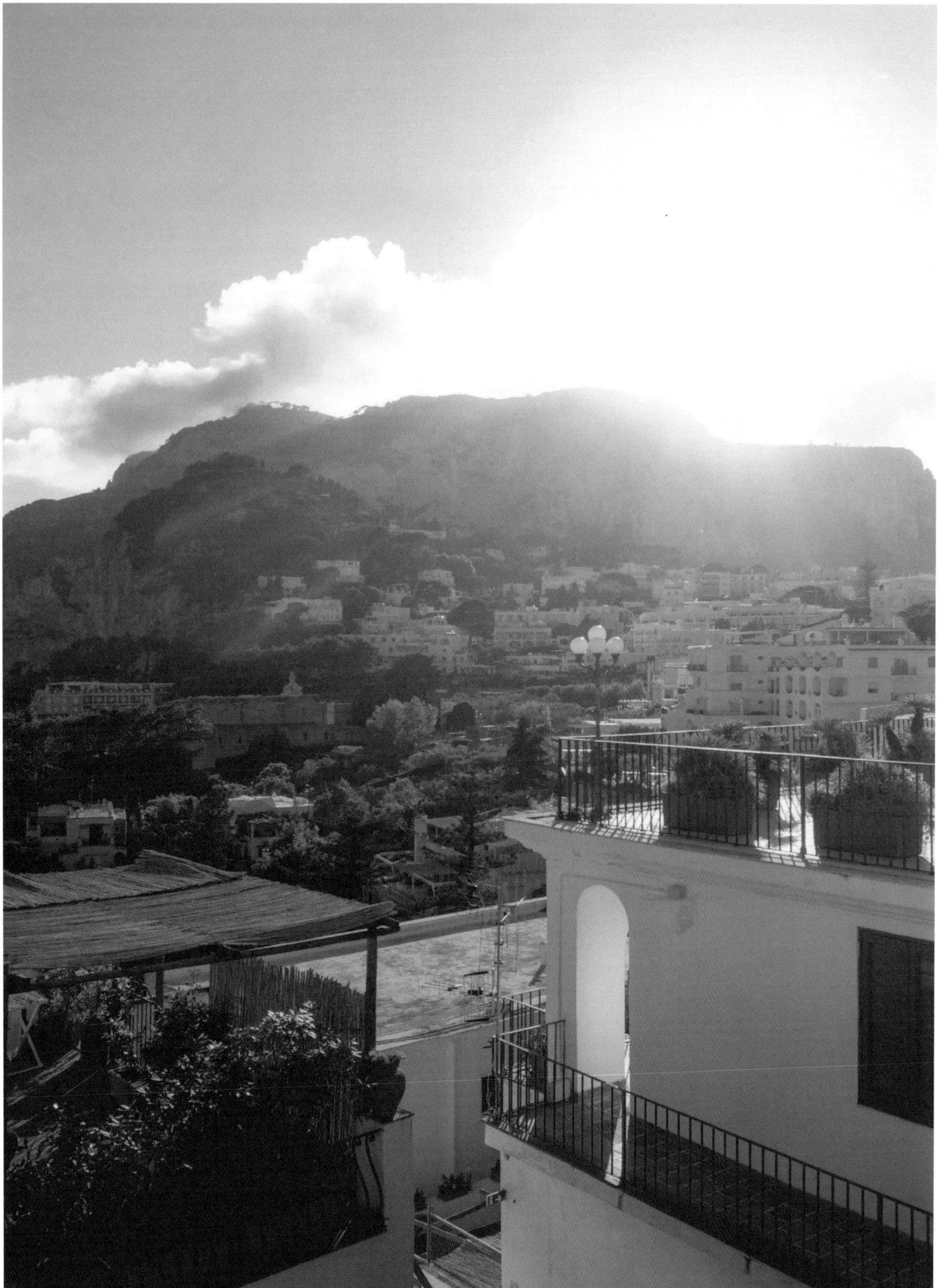

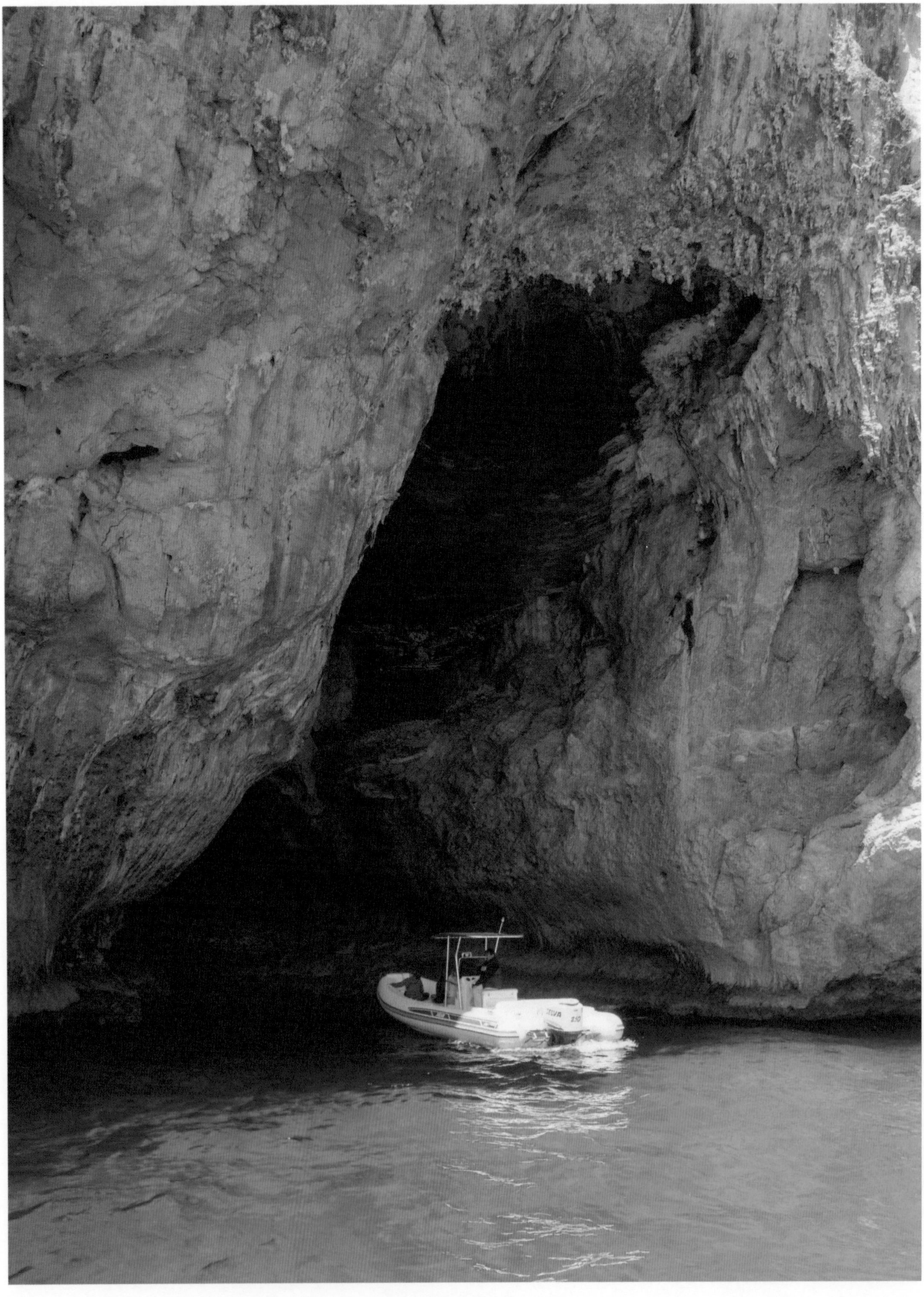

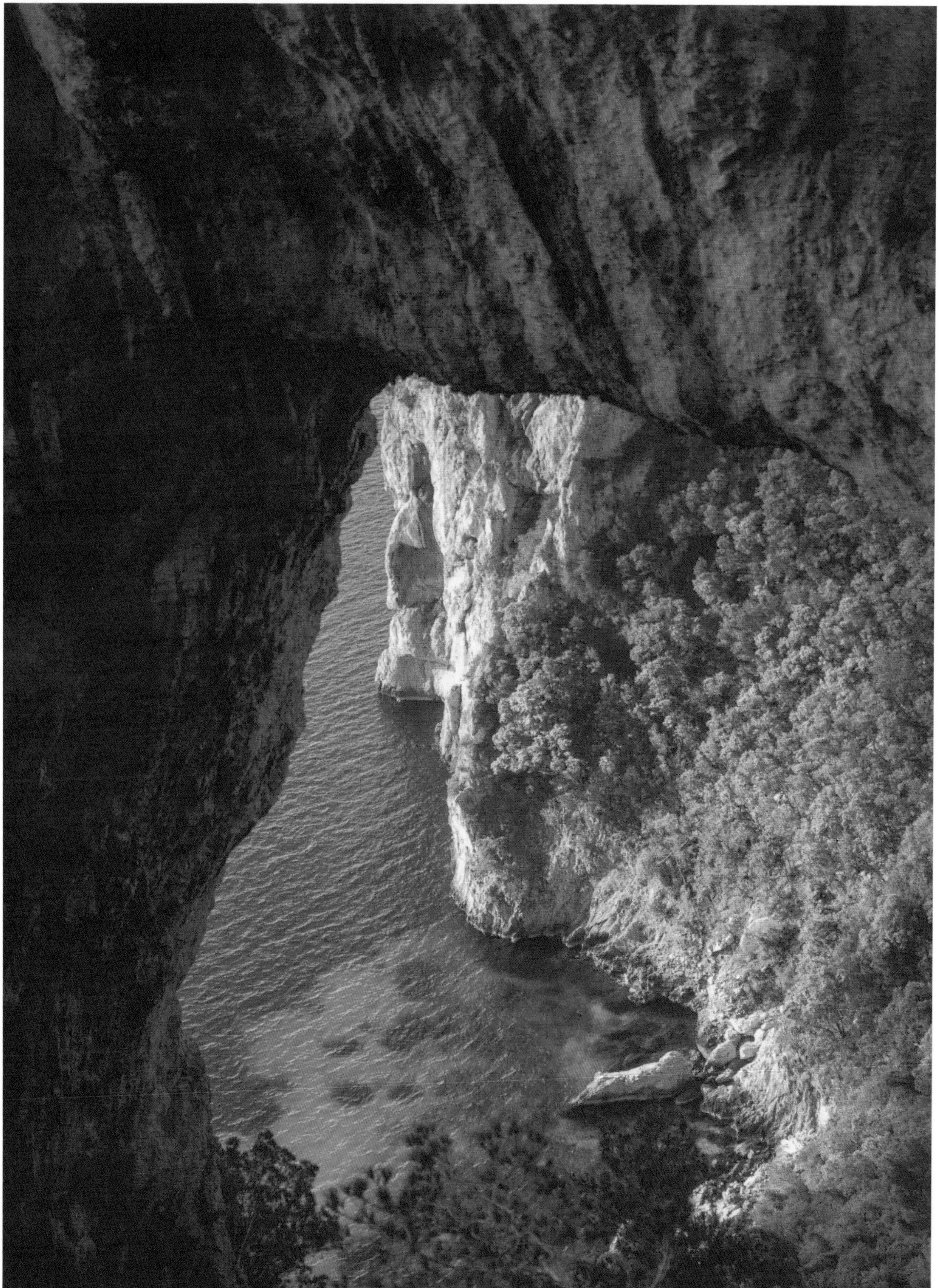

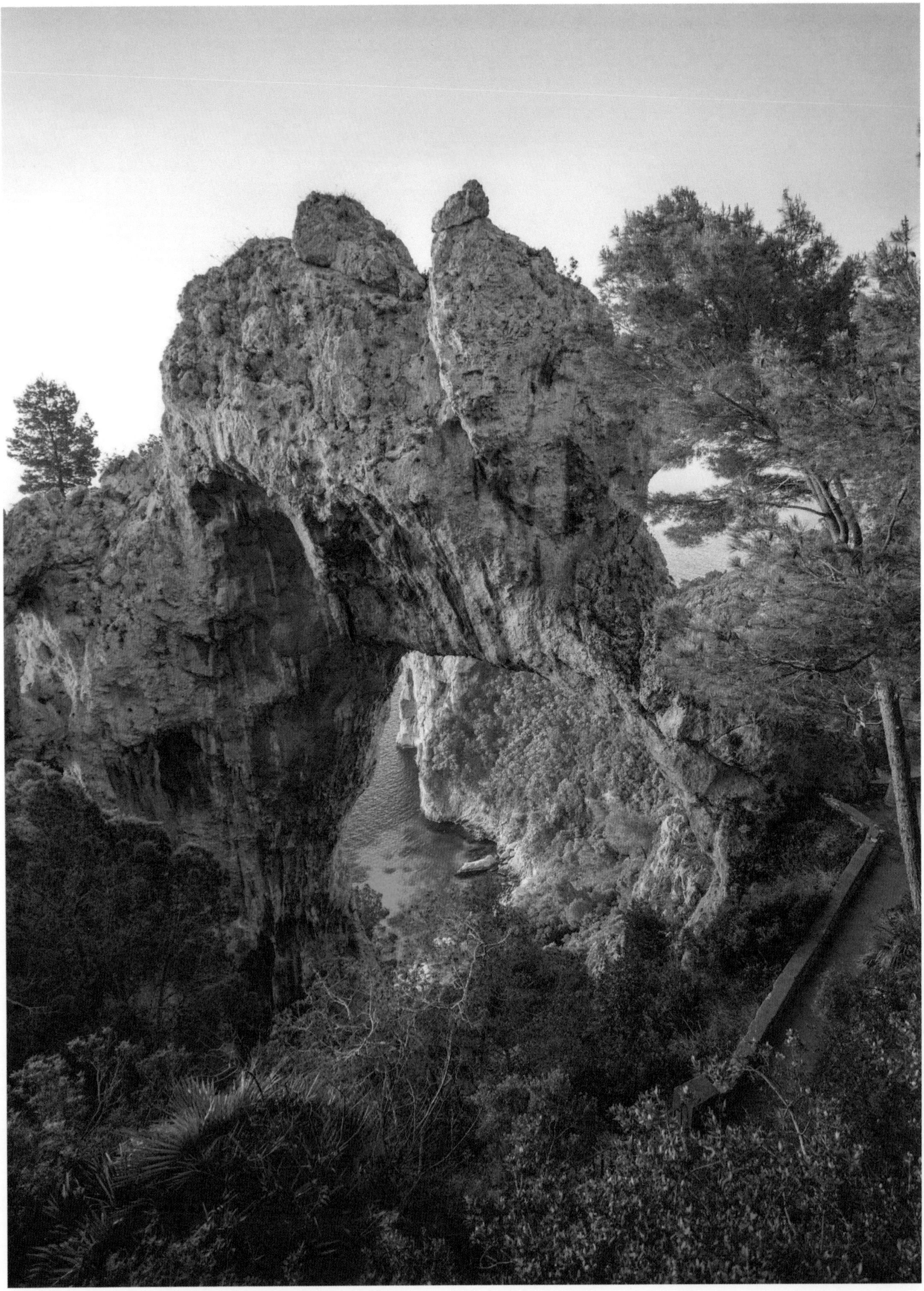

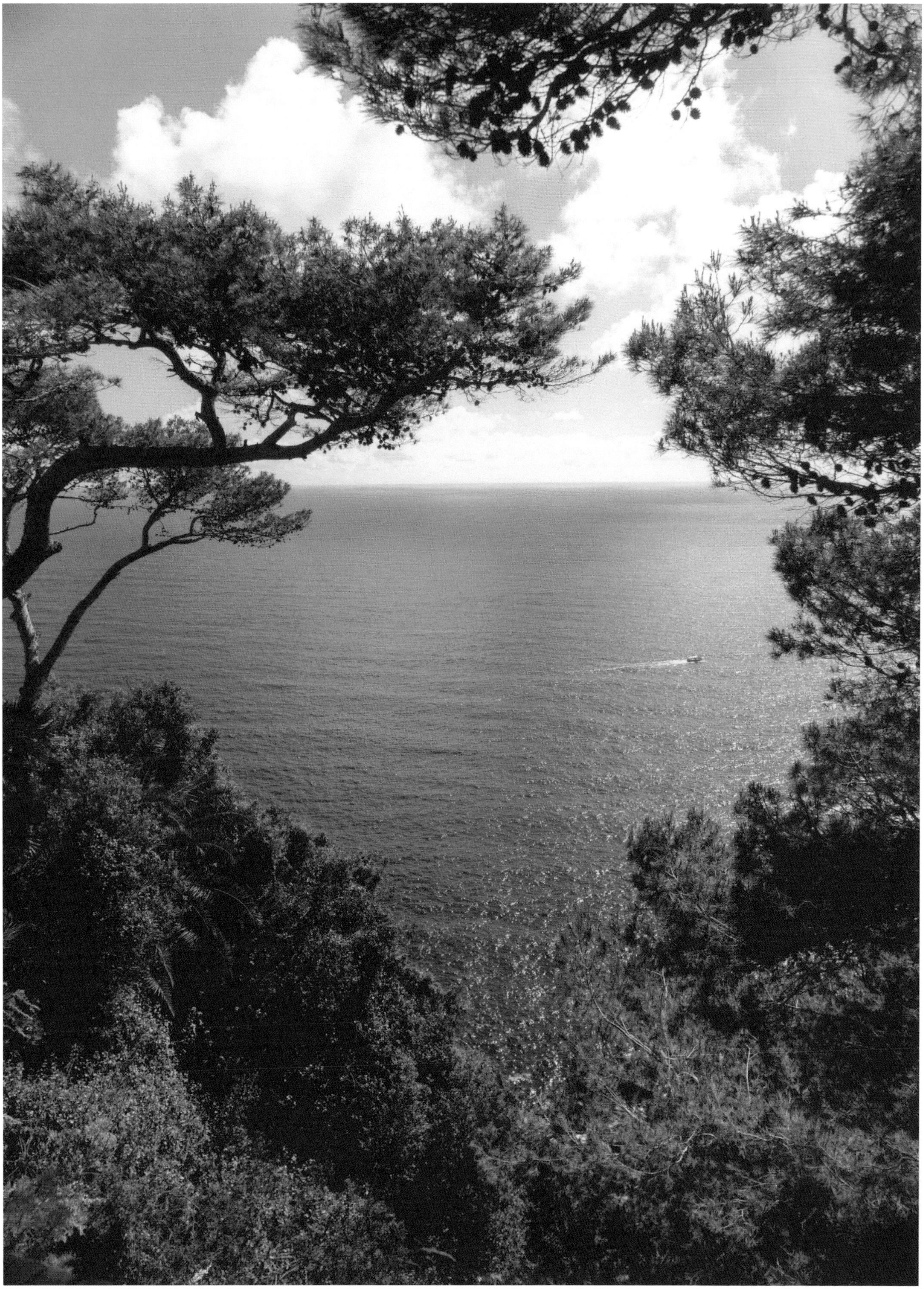

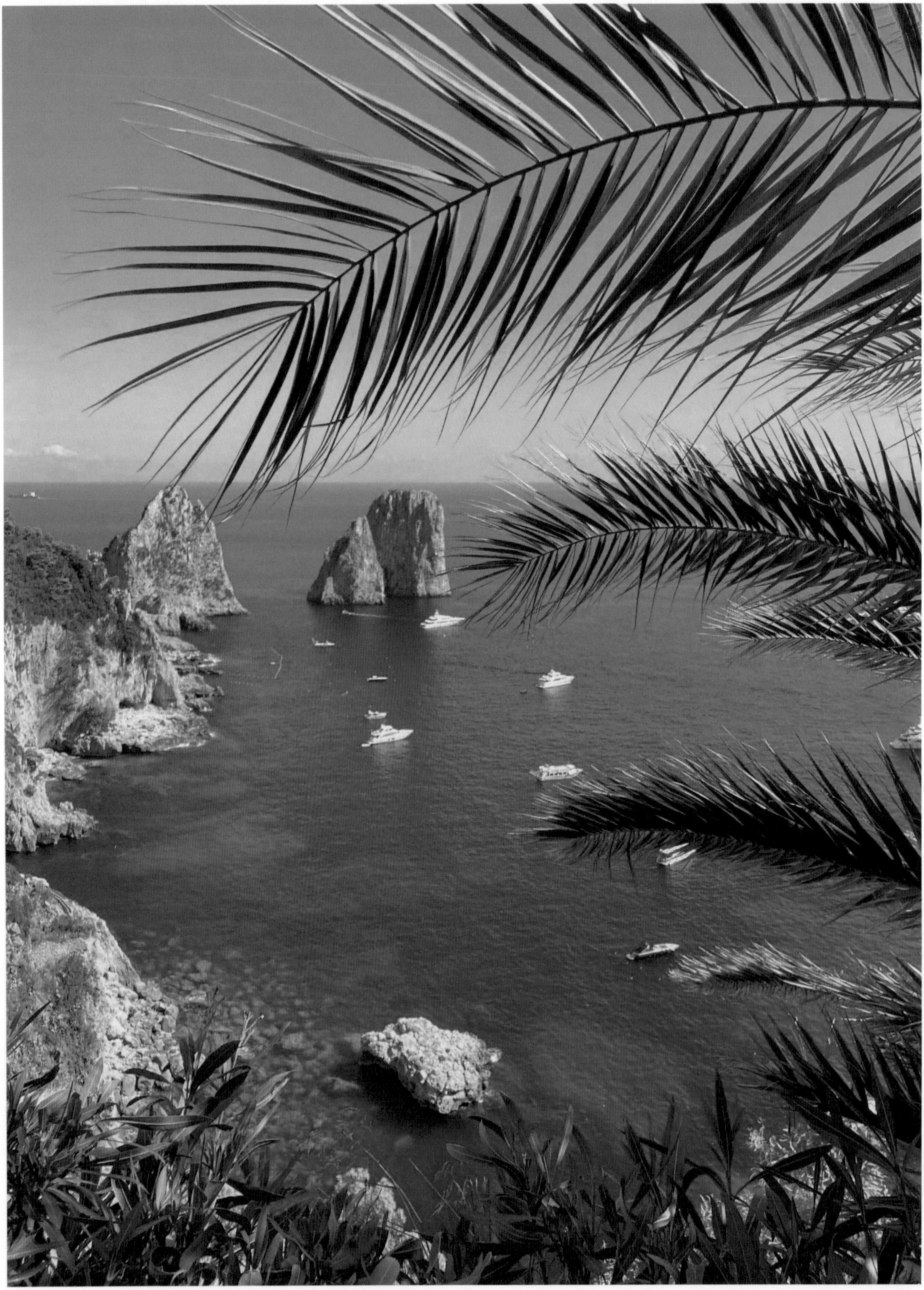

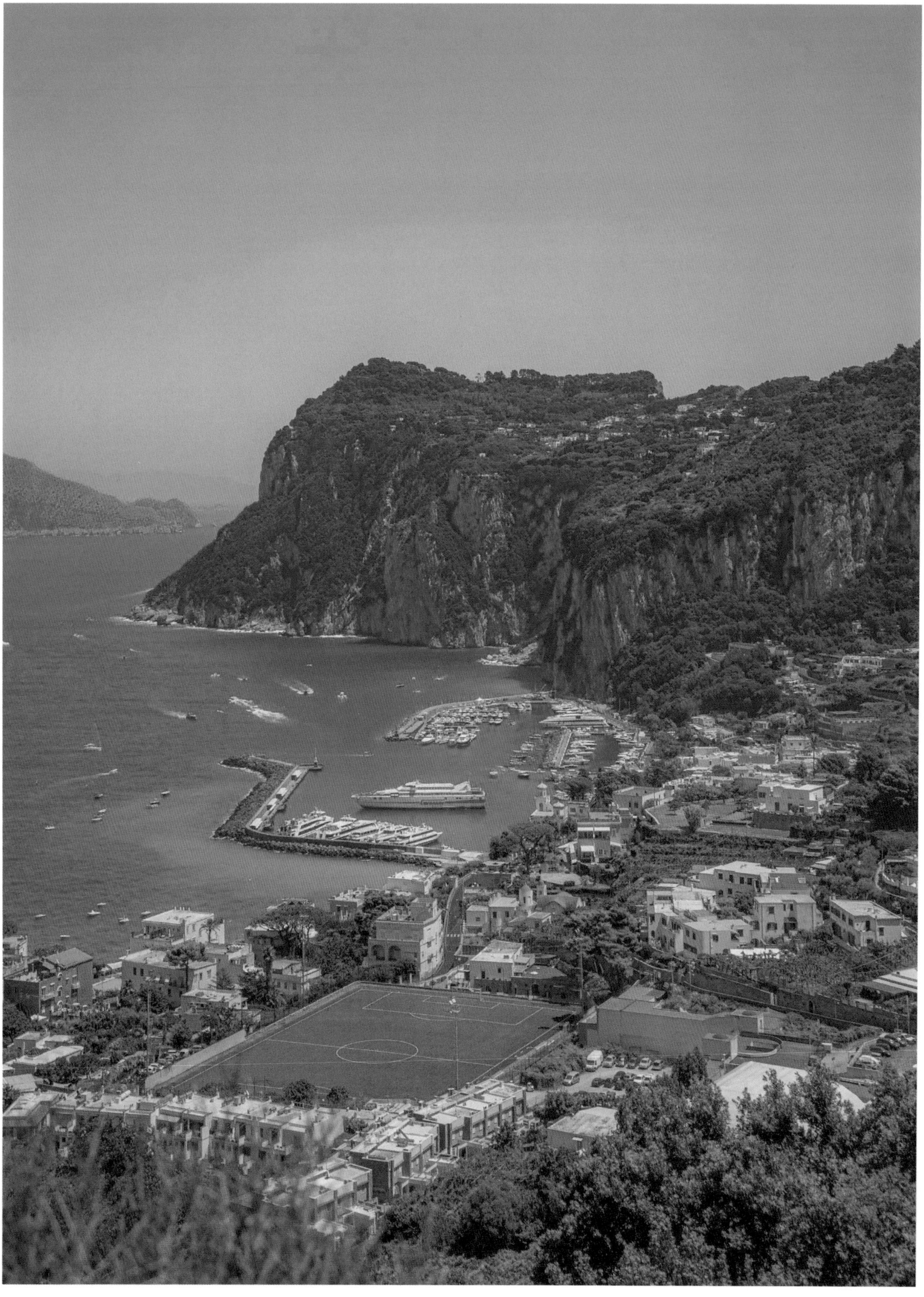

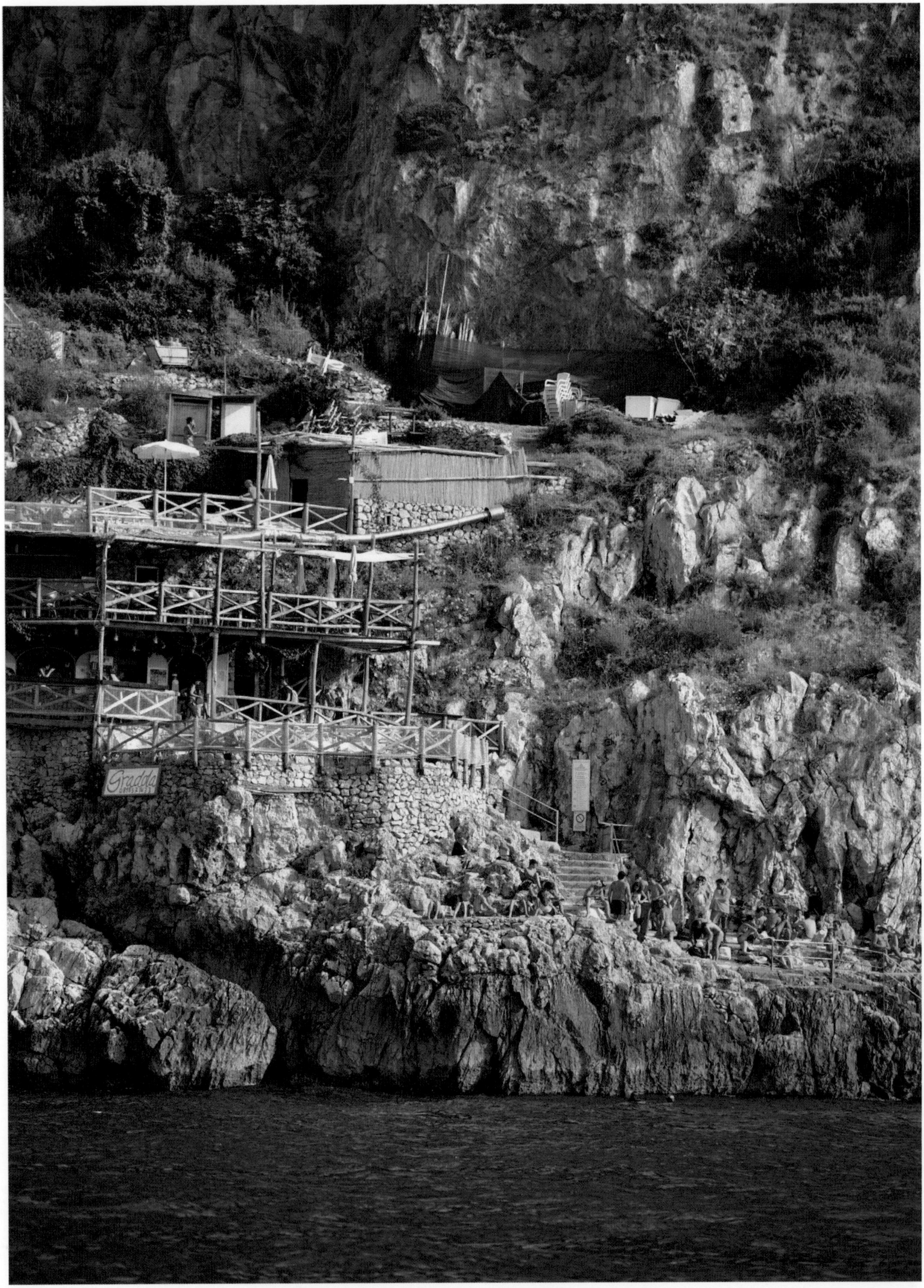
Gradola

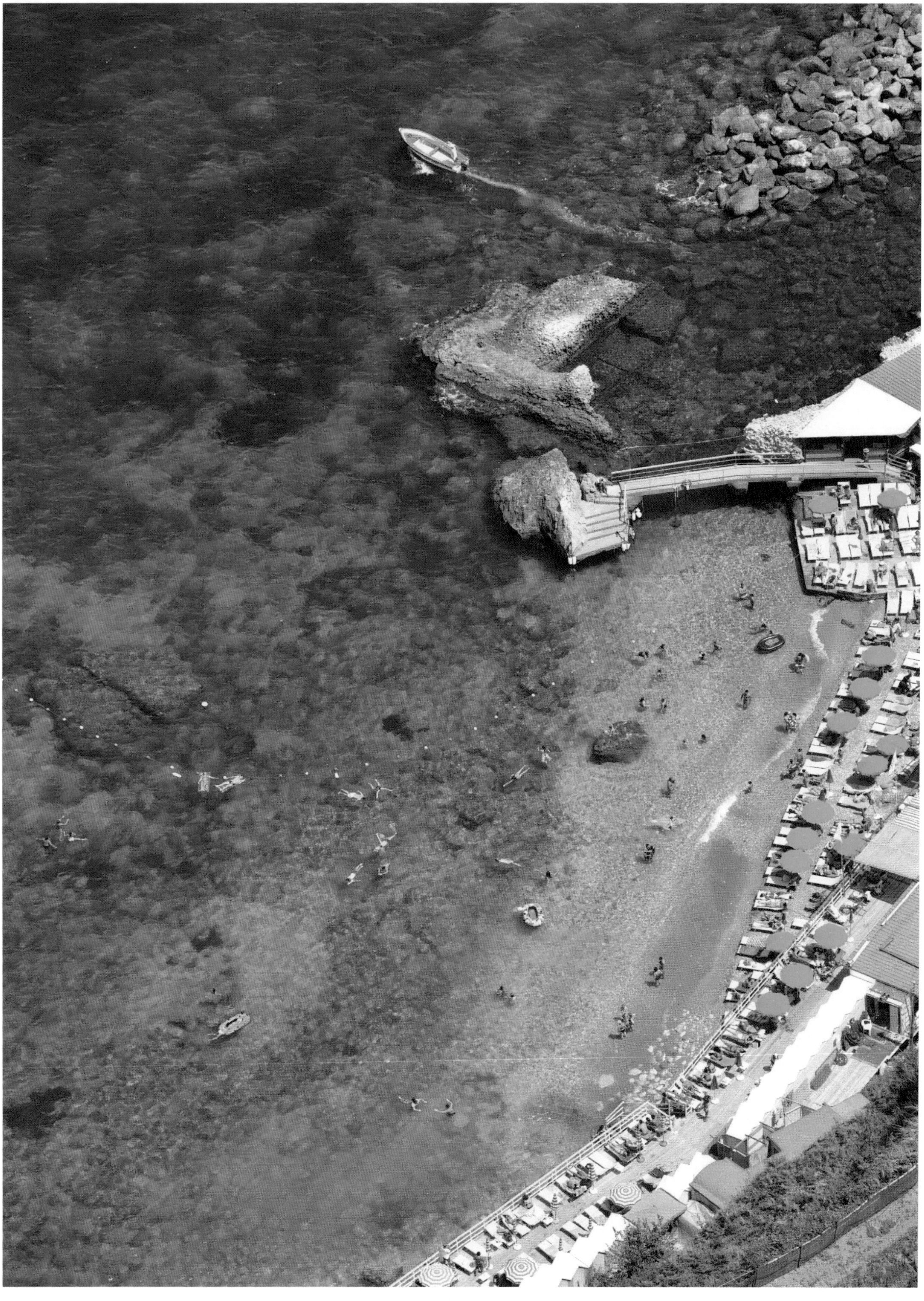

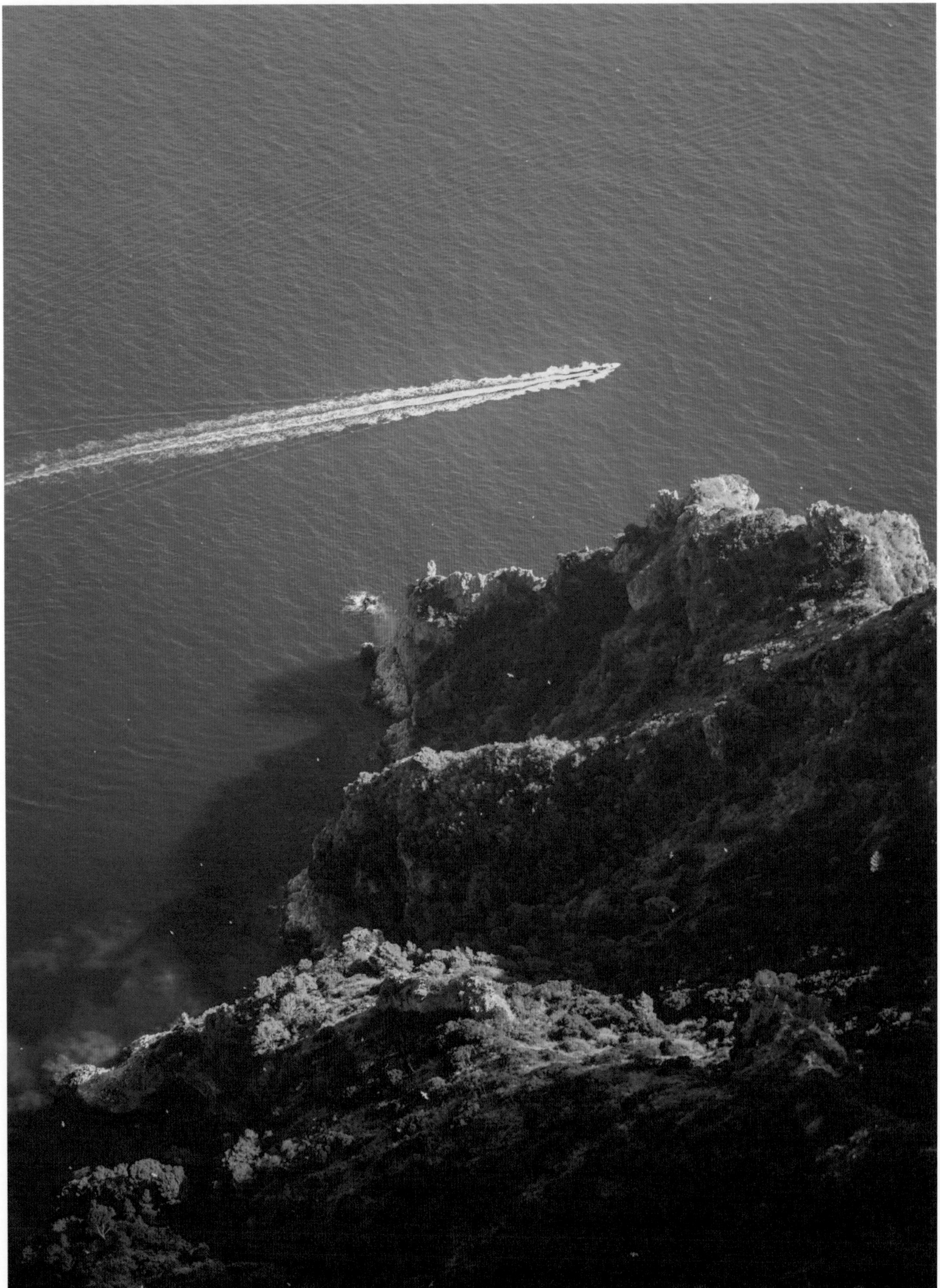

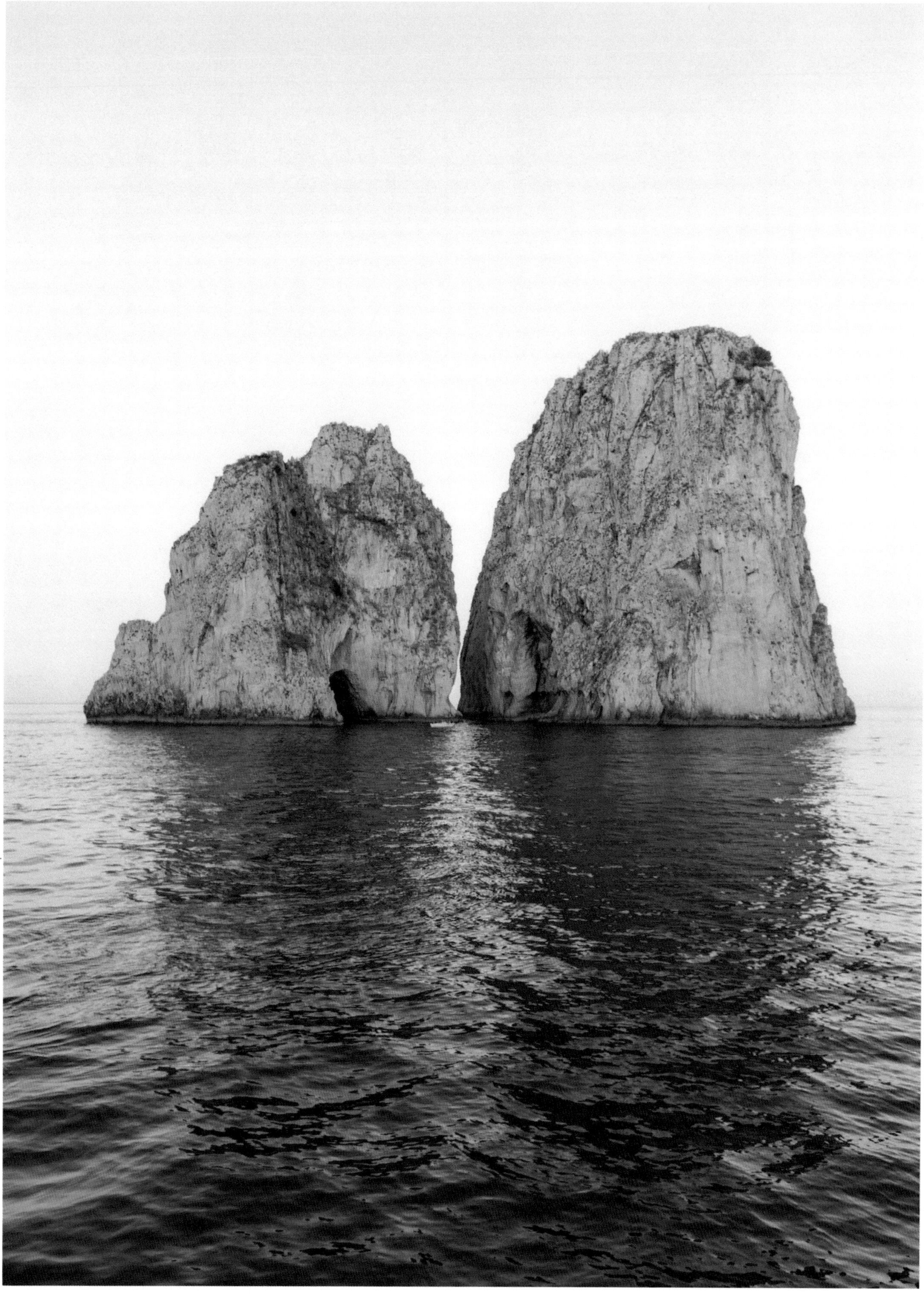

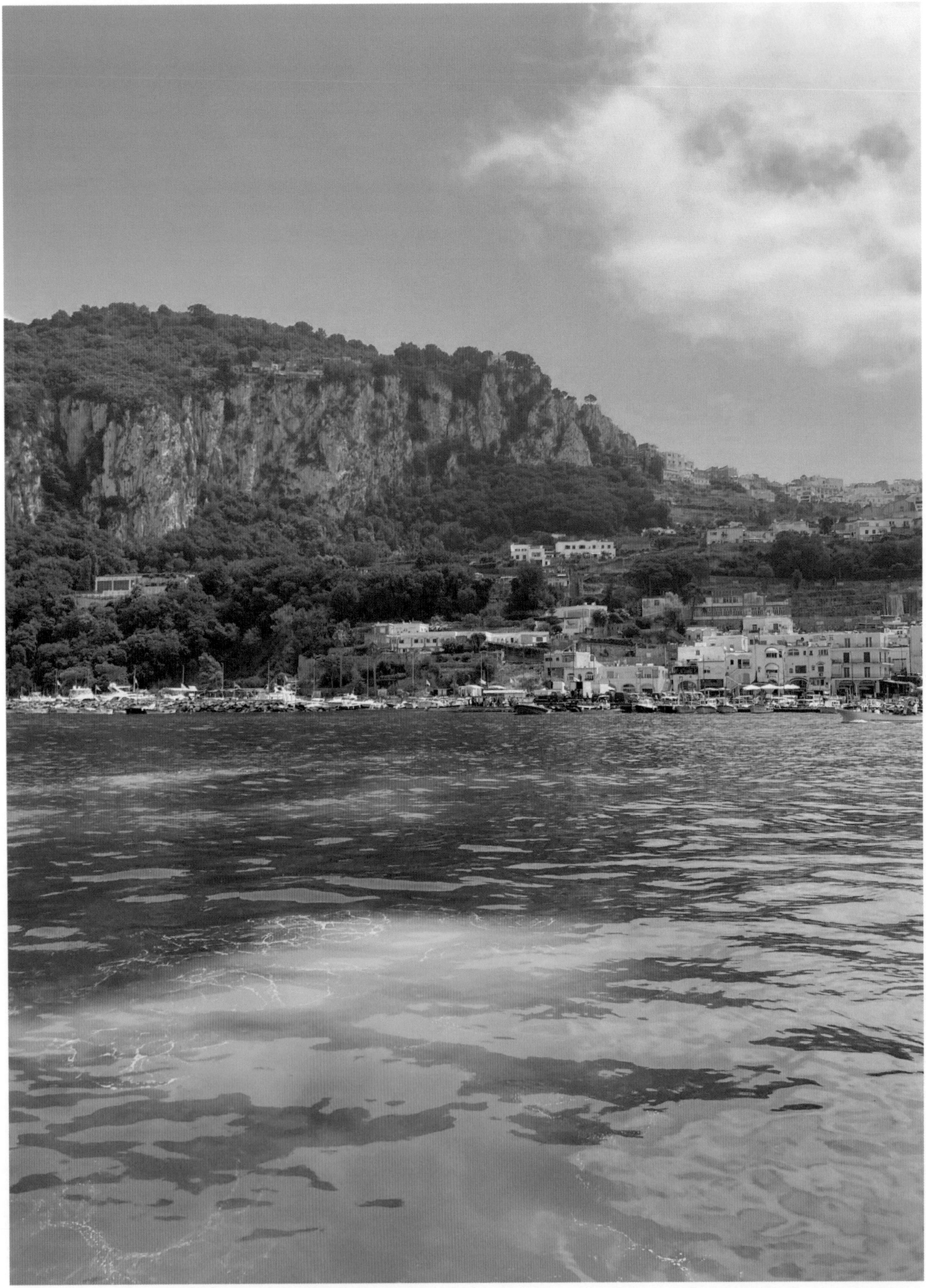

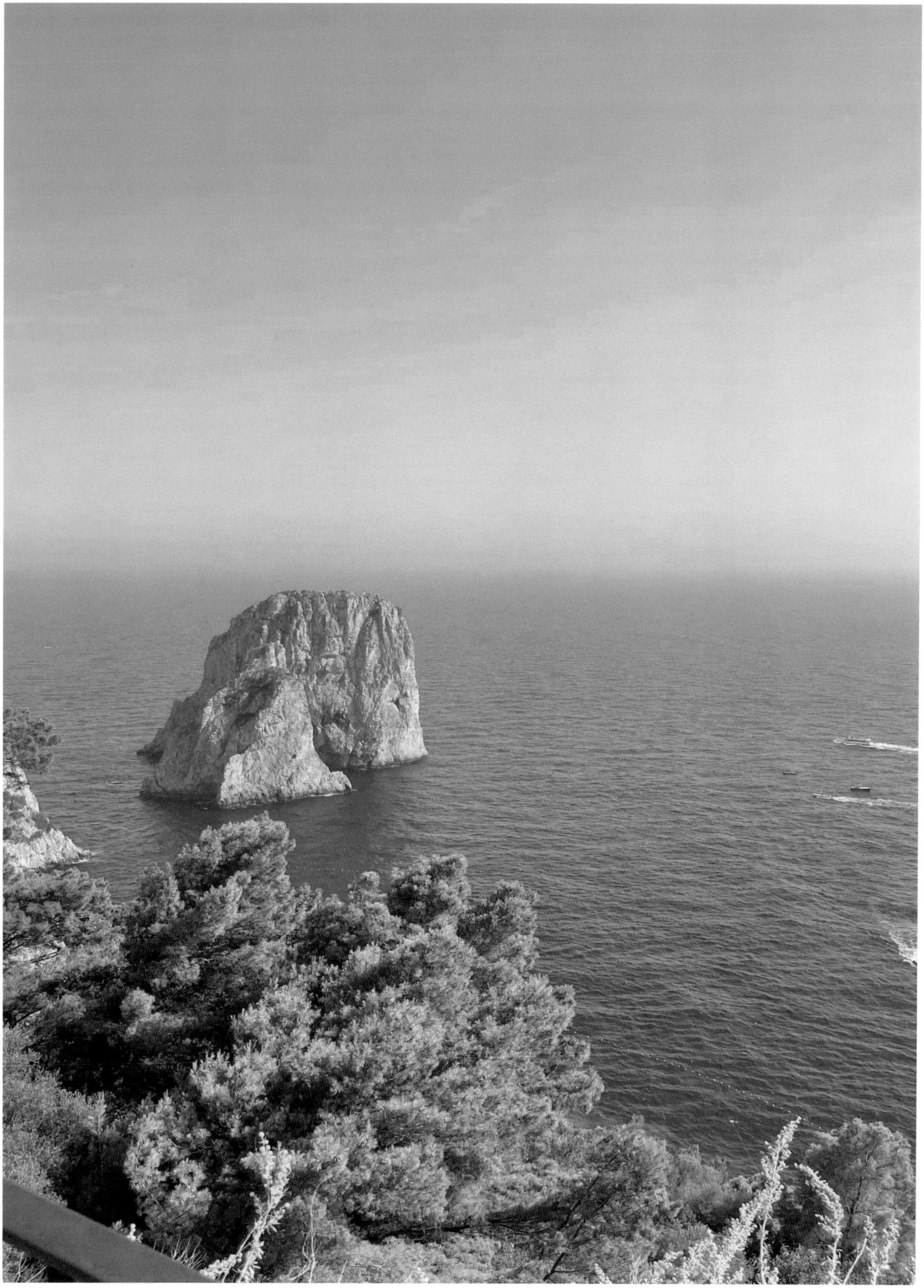

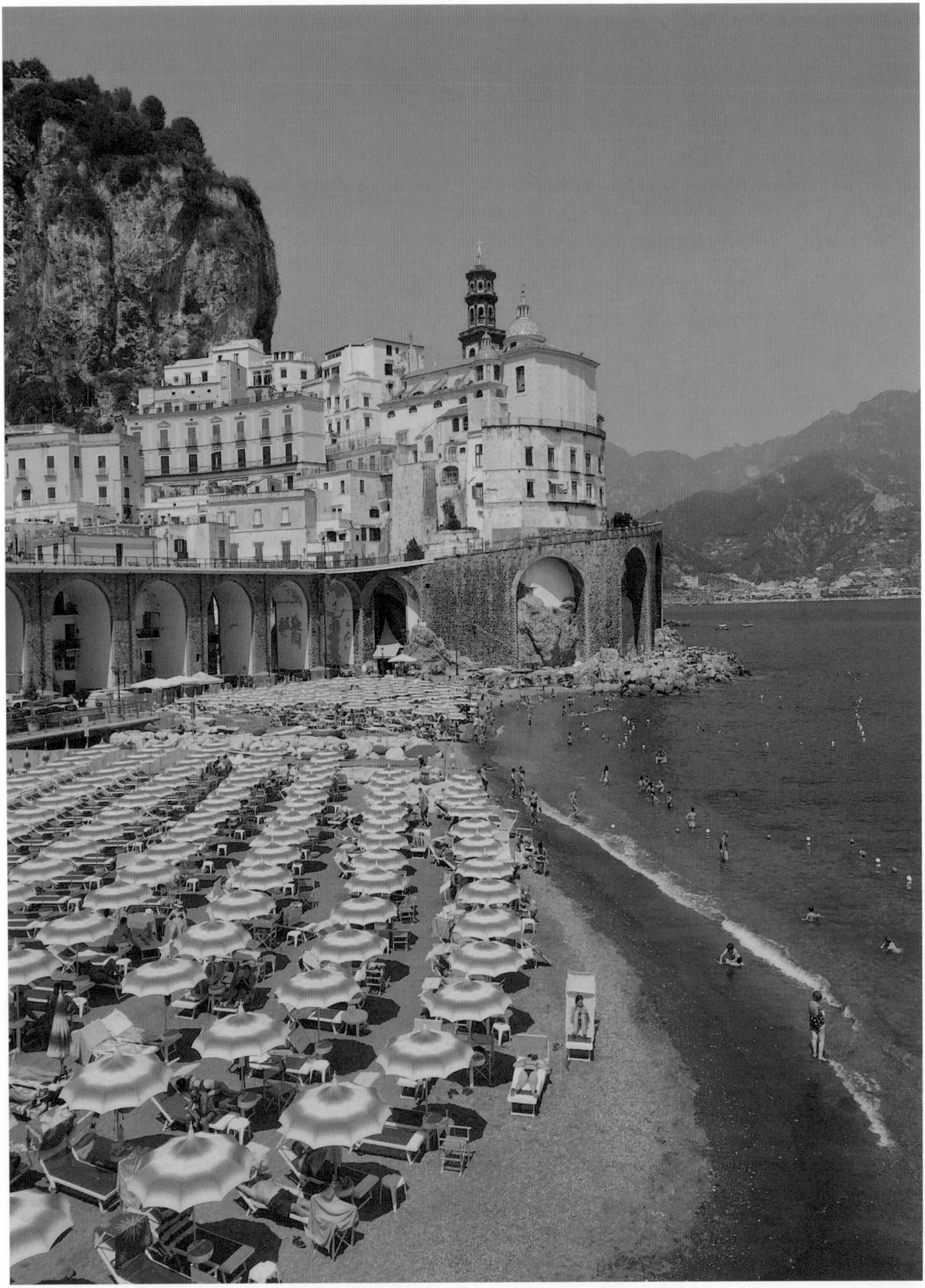

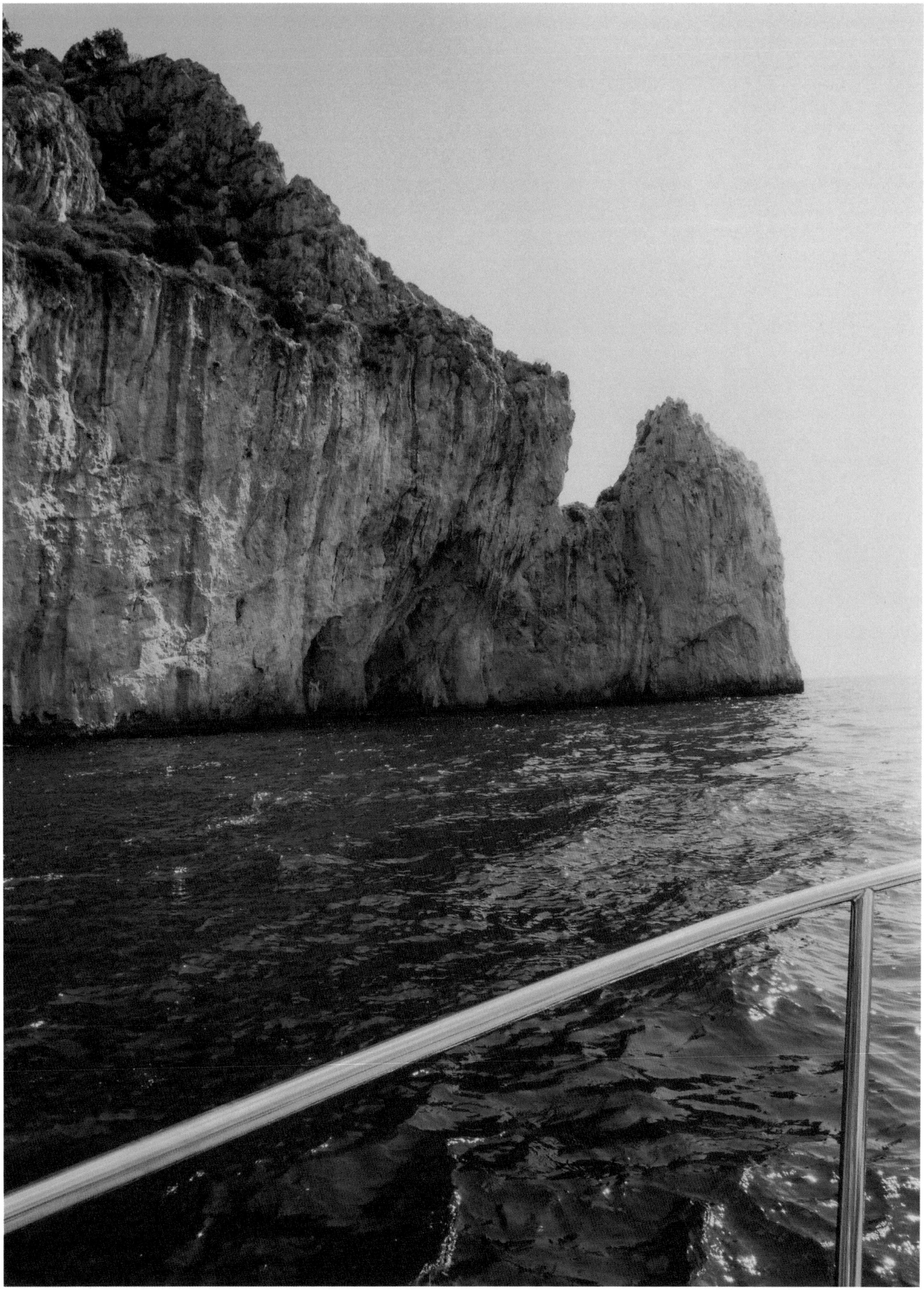

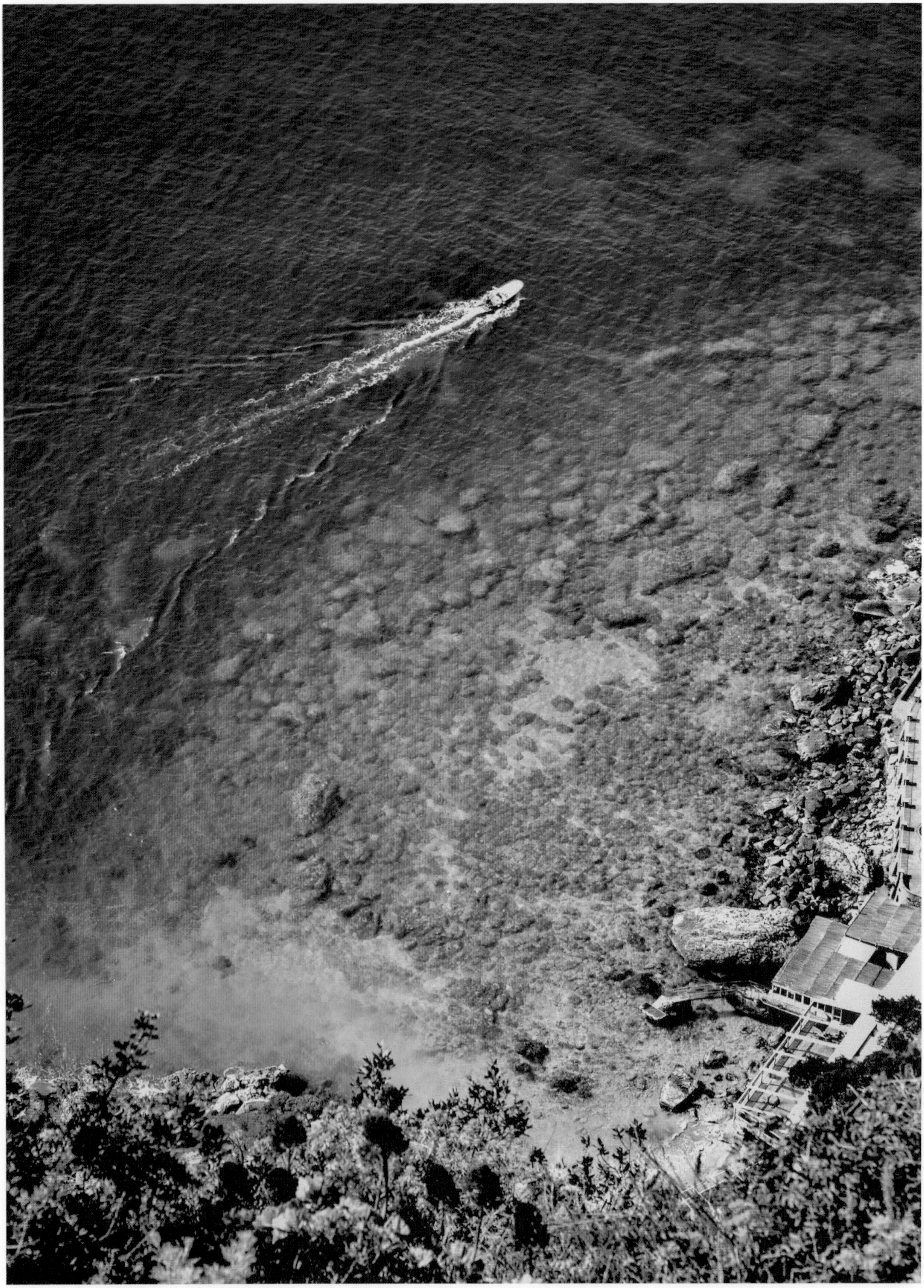

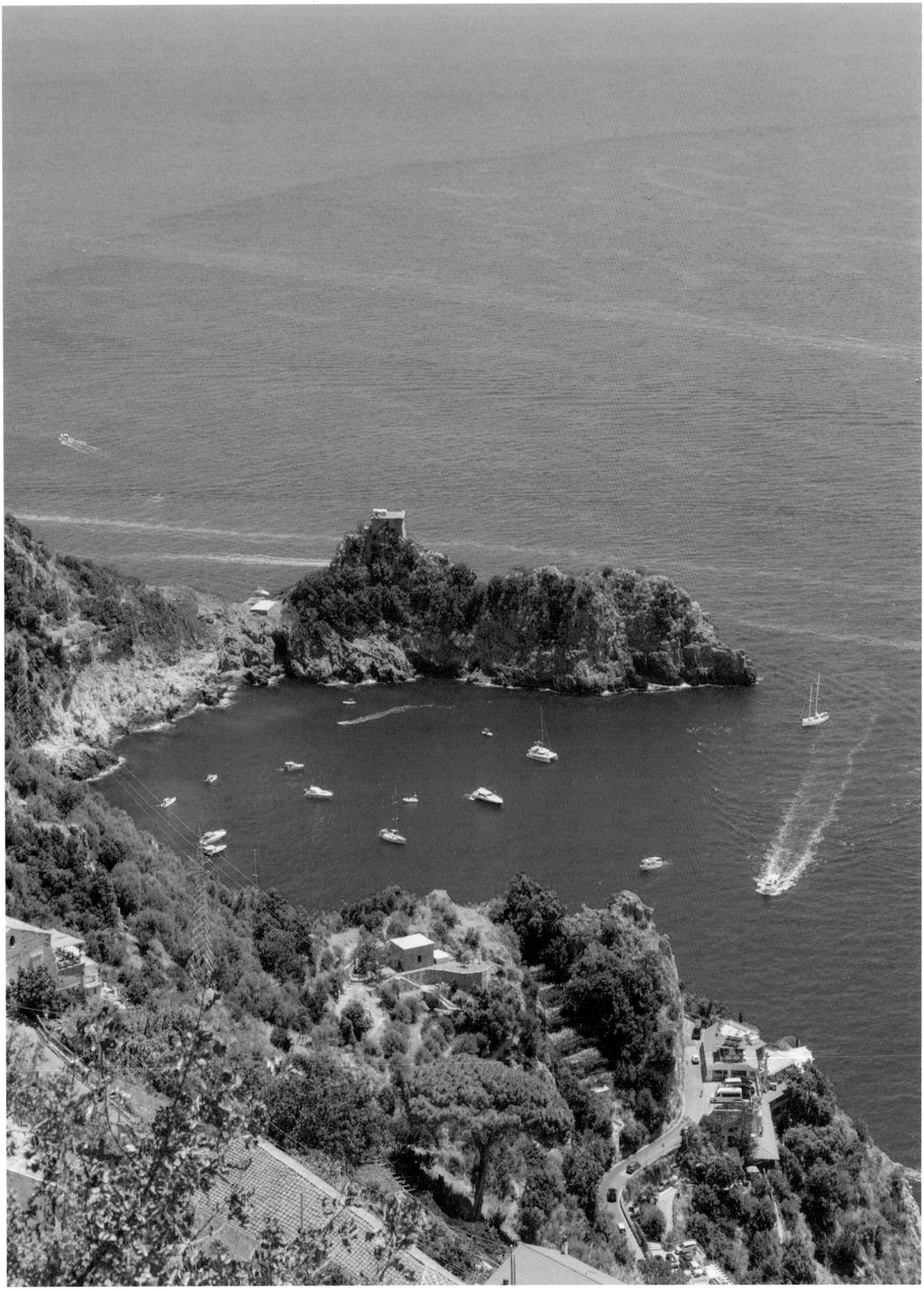

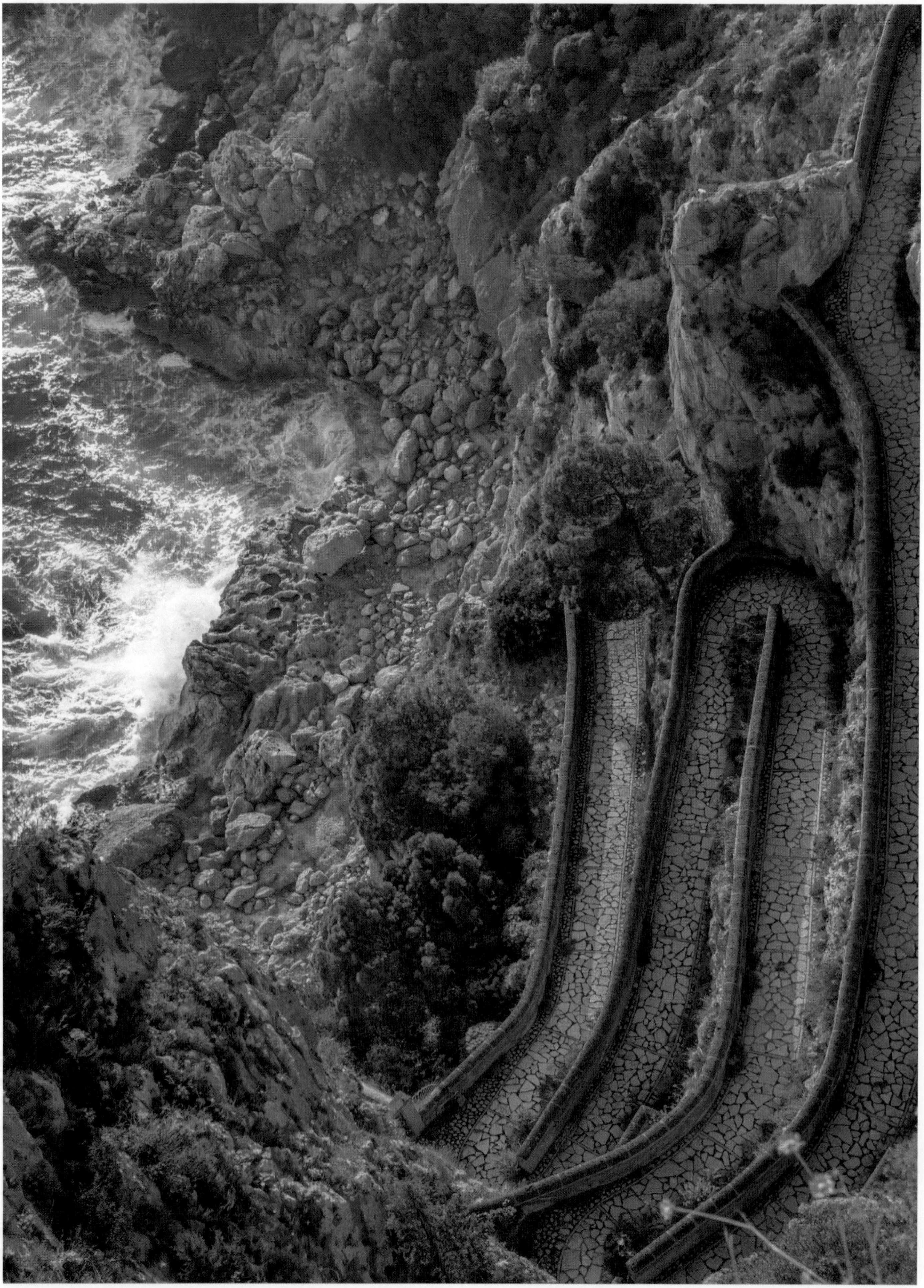

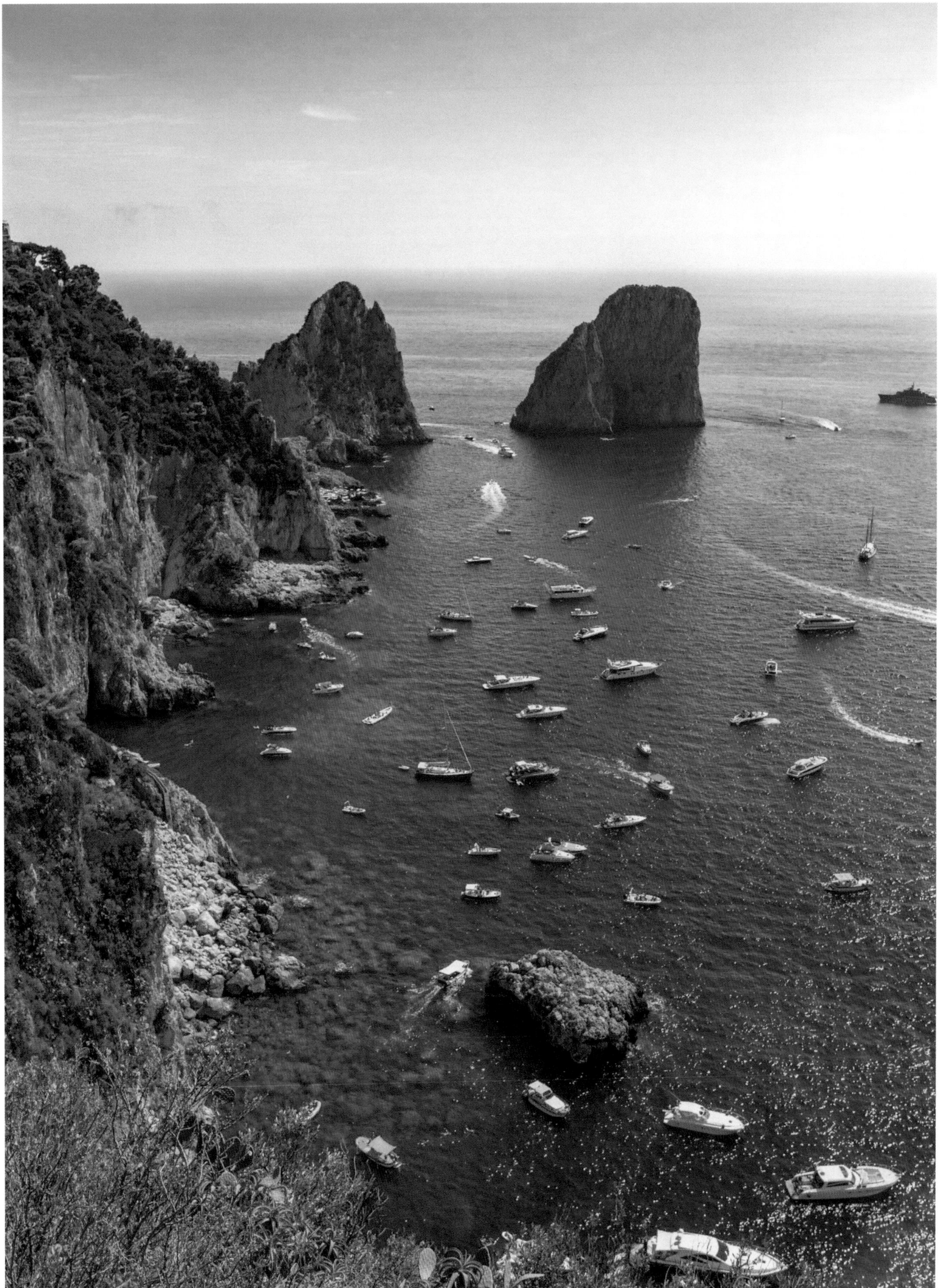

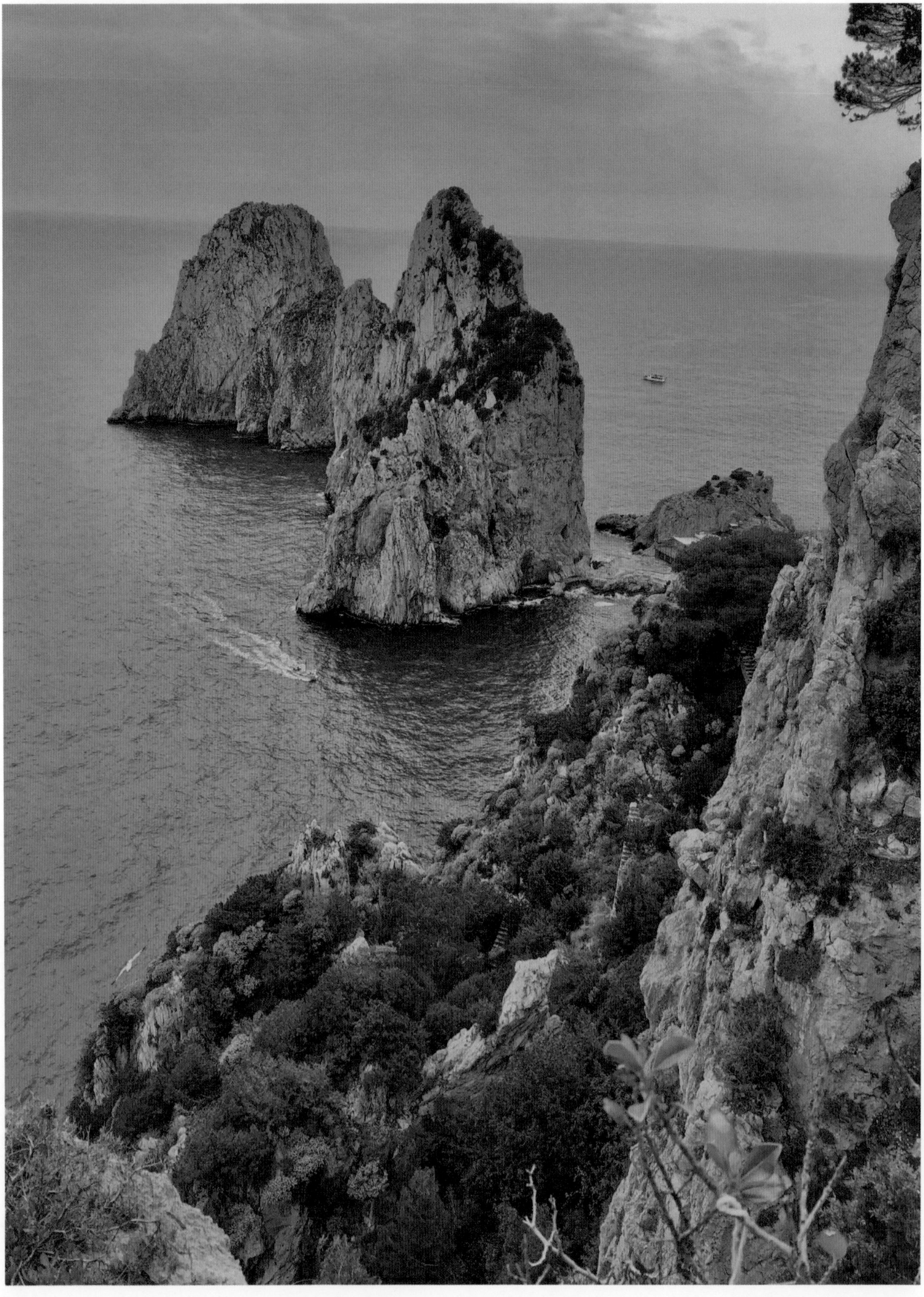

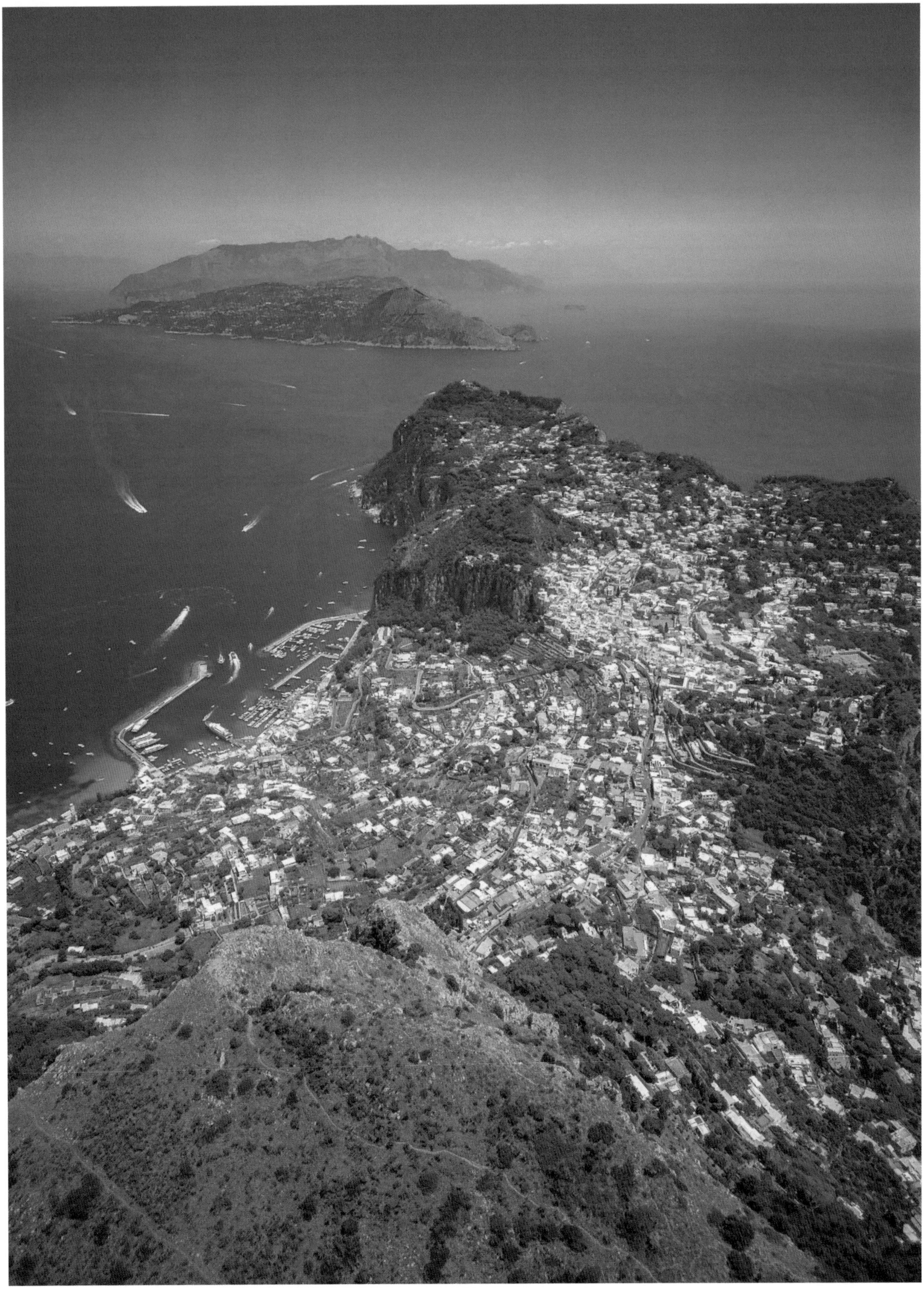

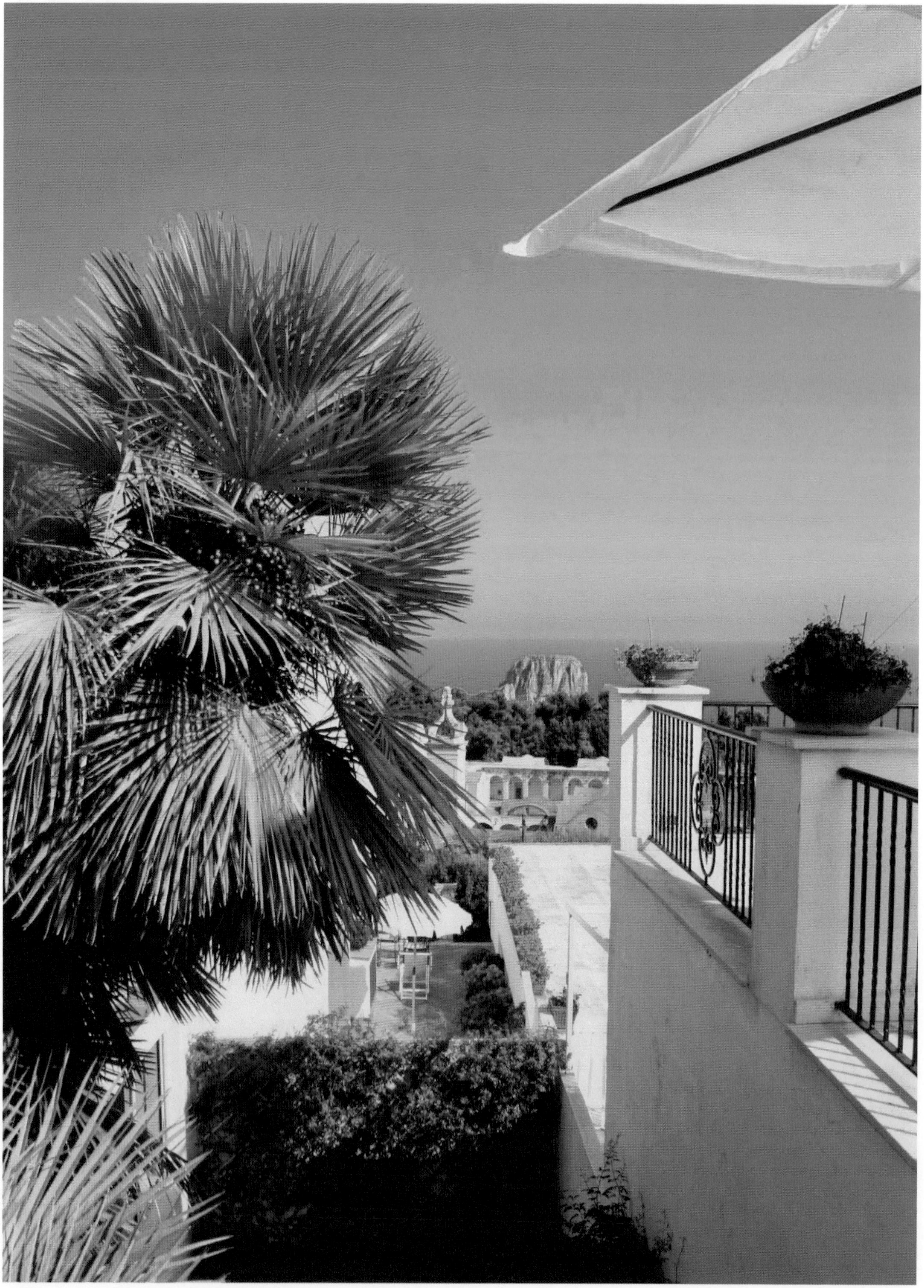

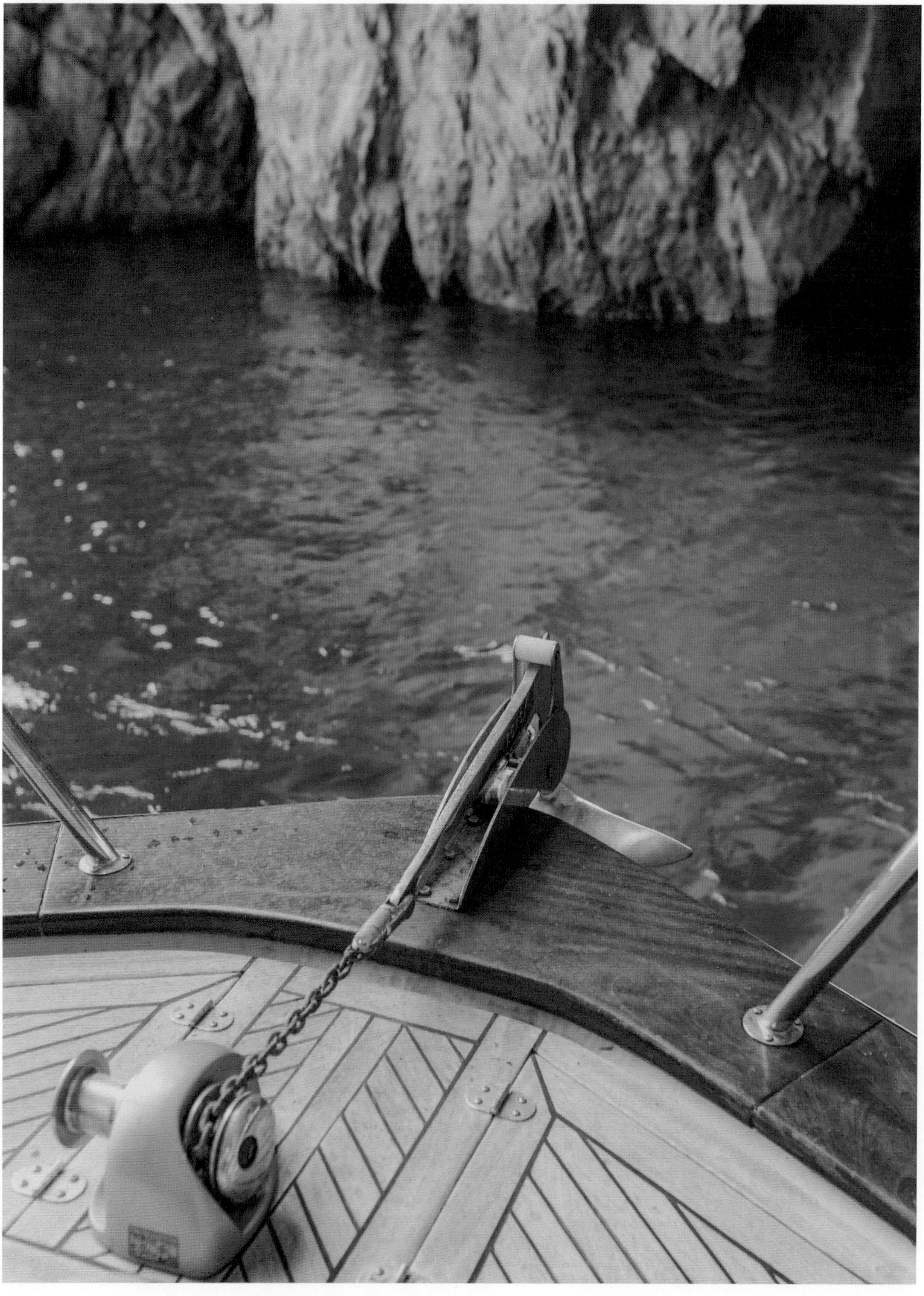

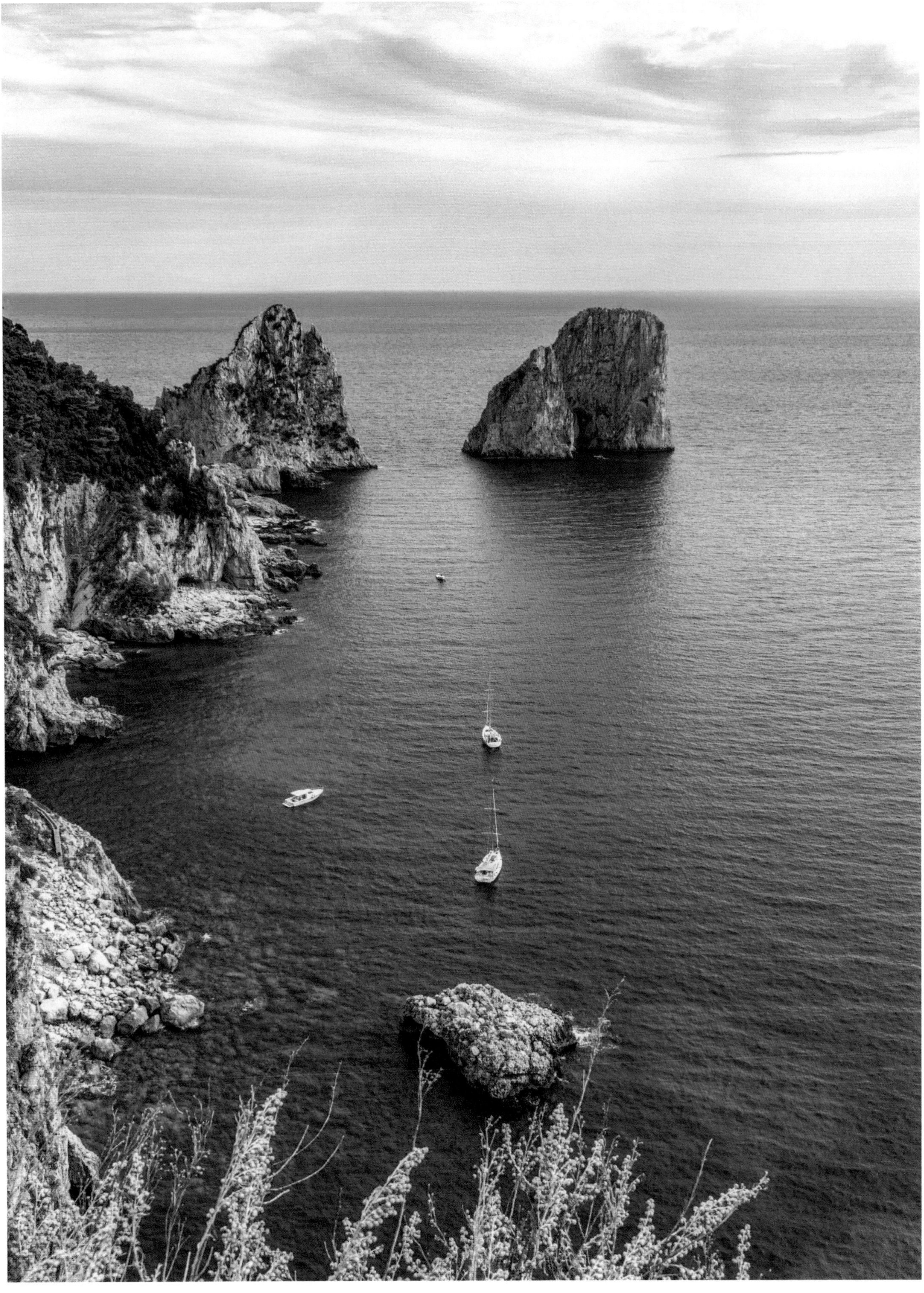

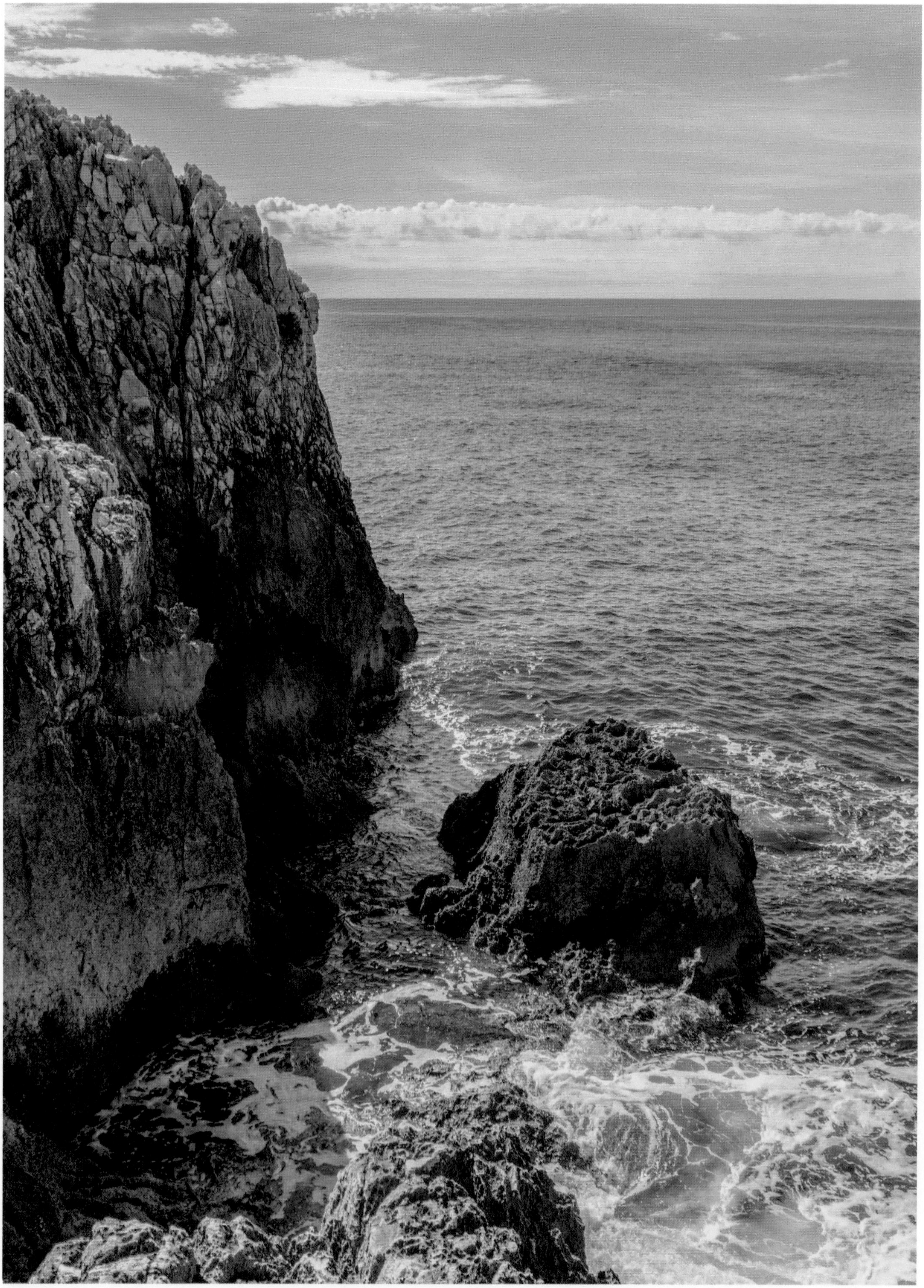

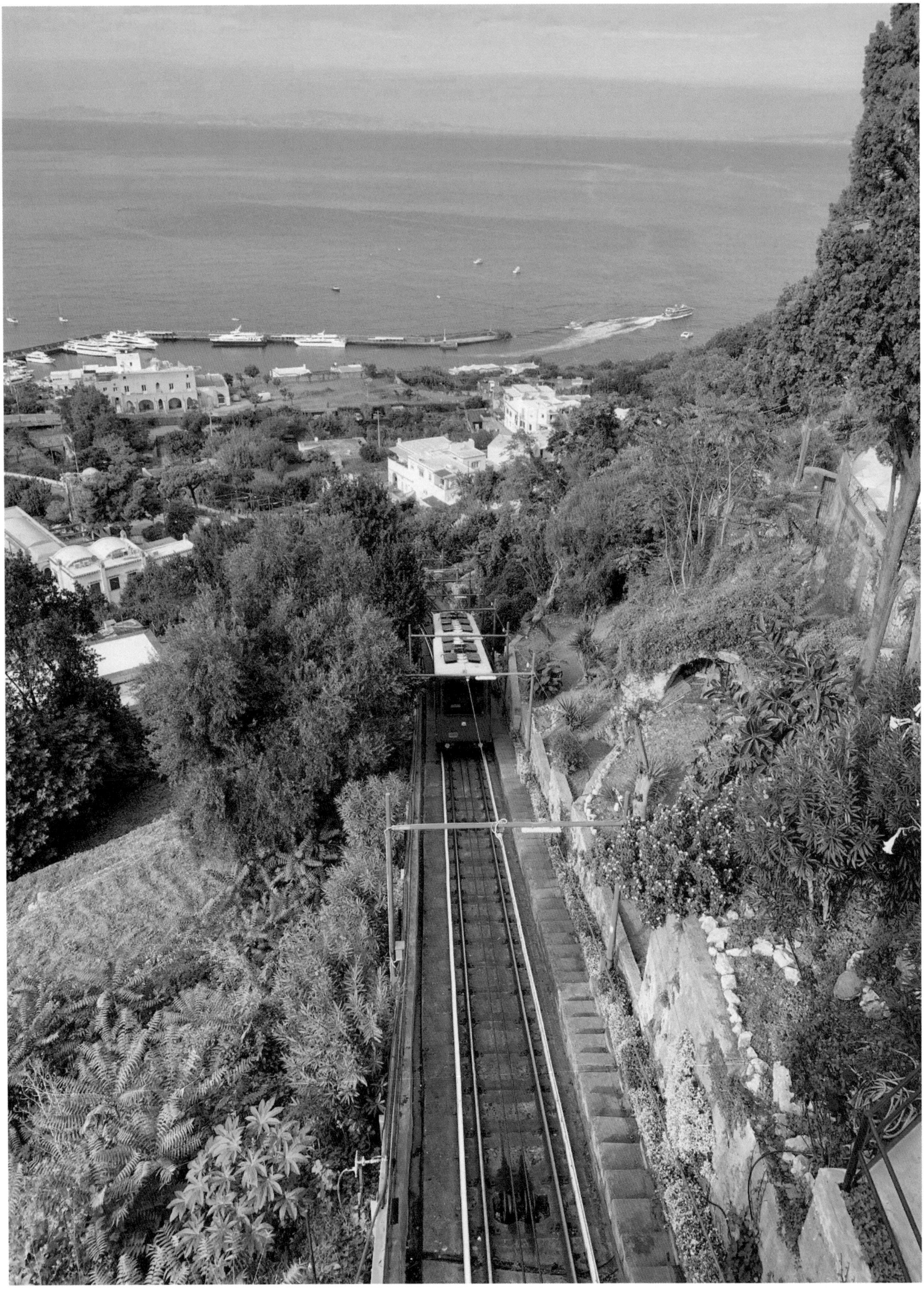

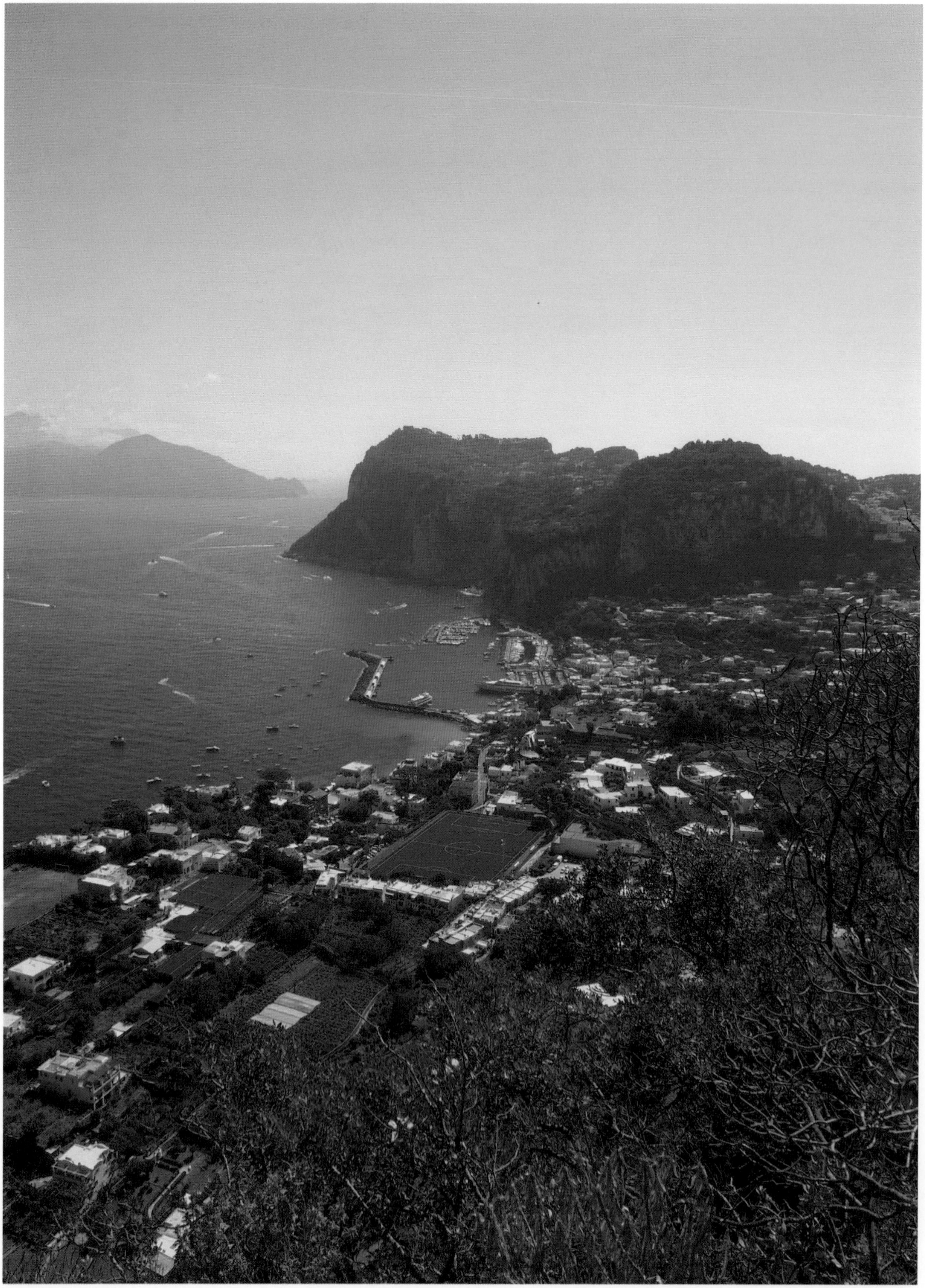

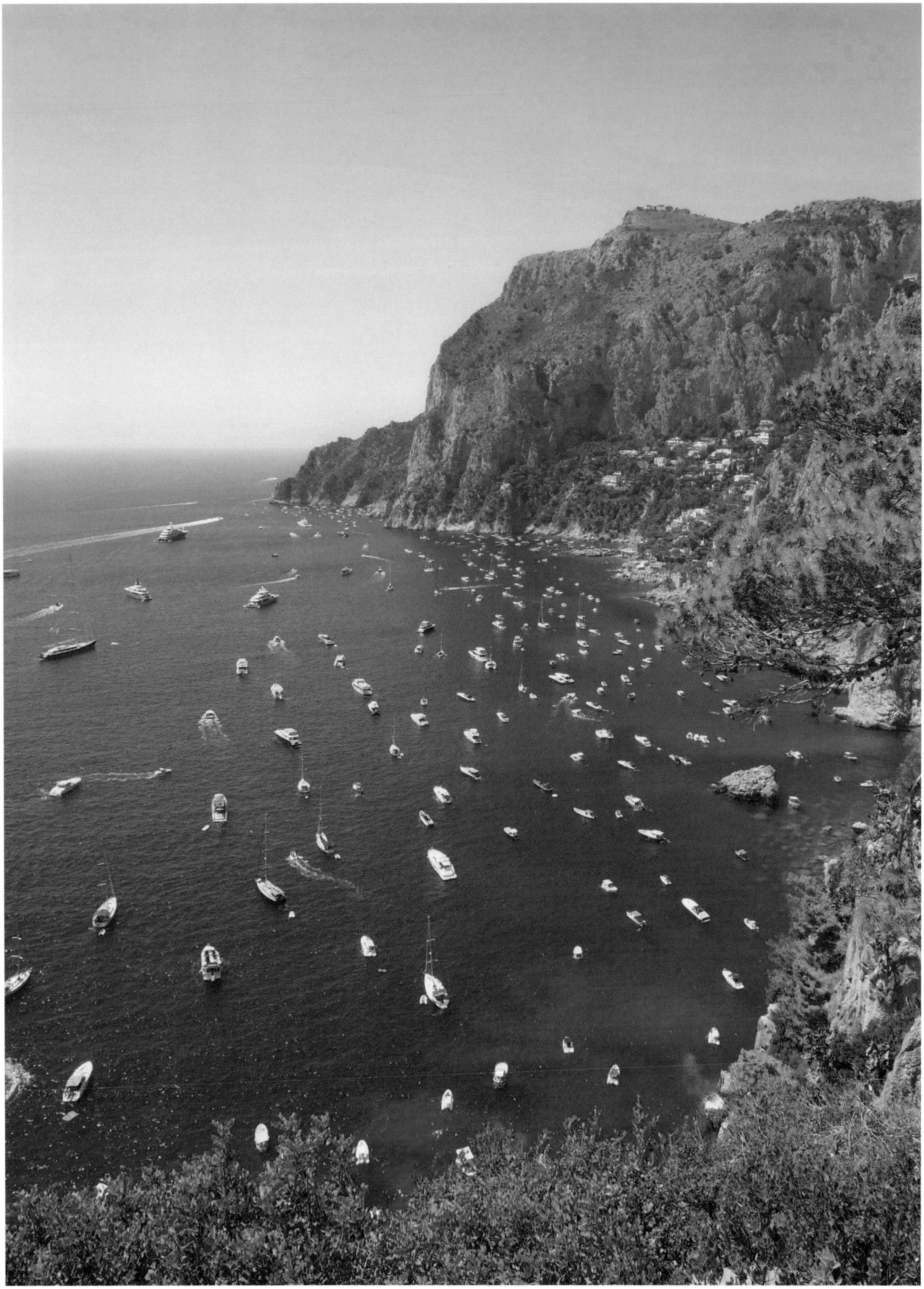

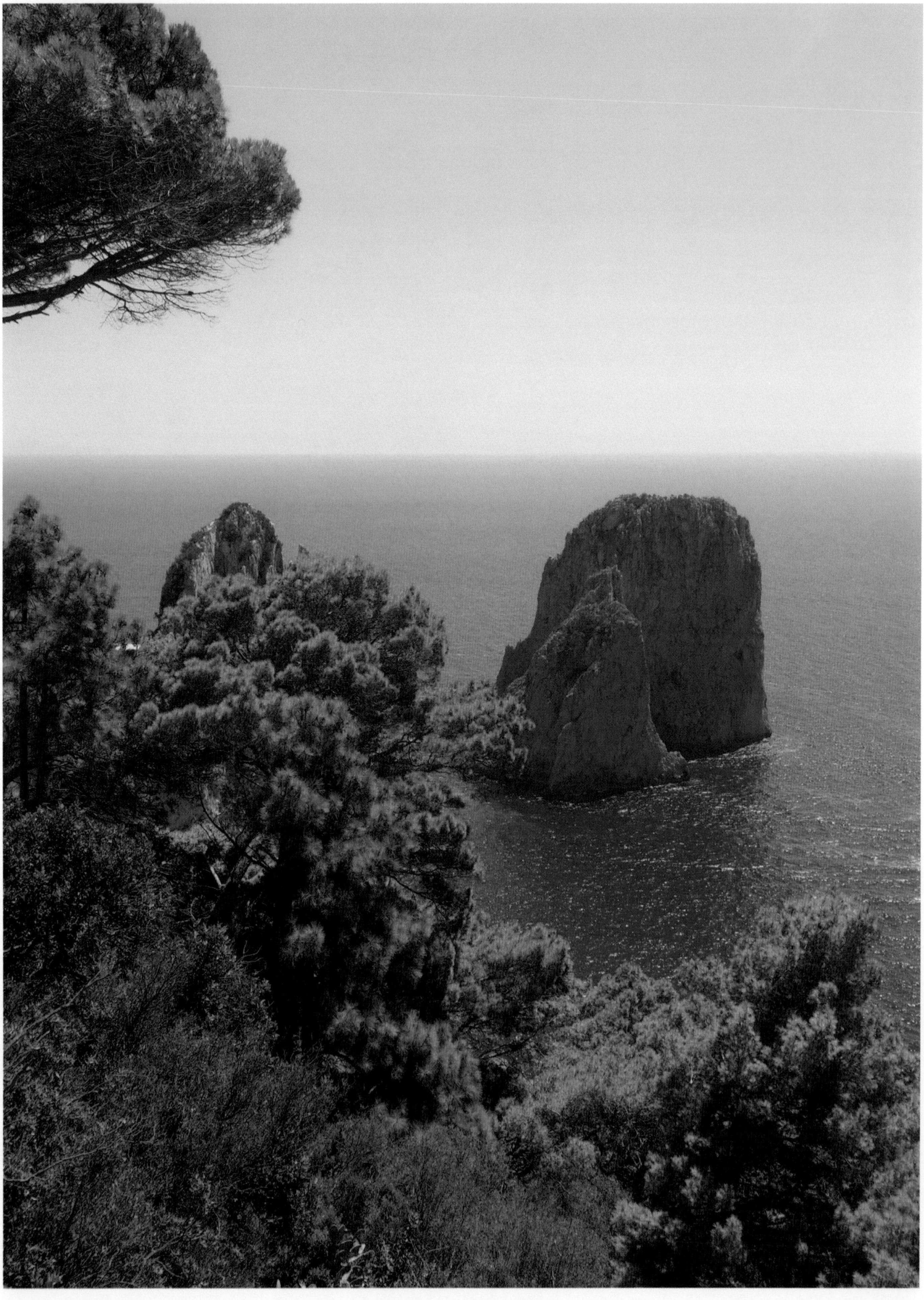

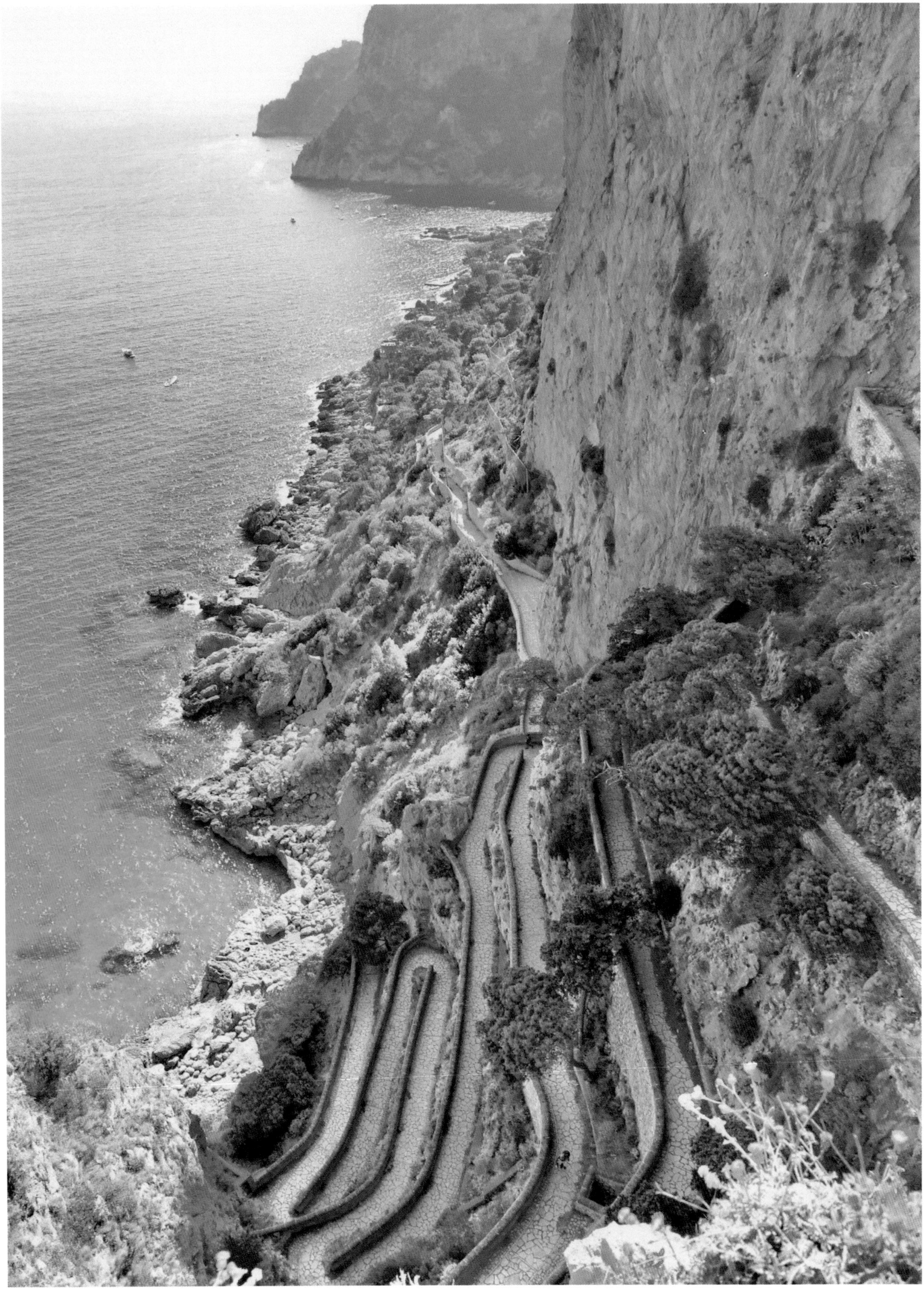

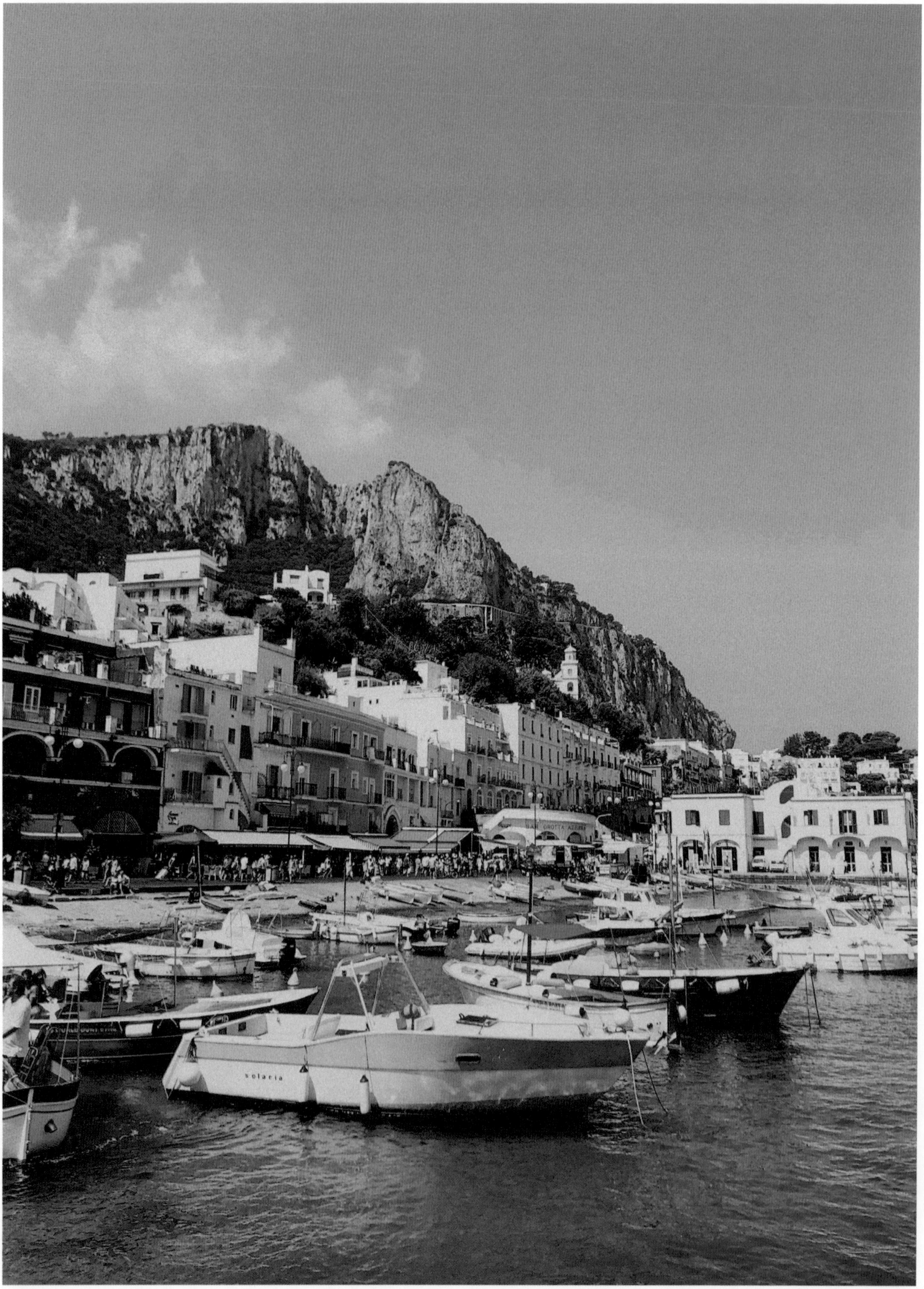
solaria

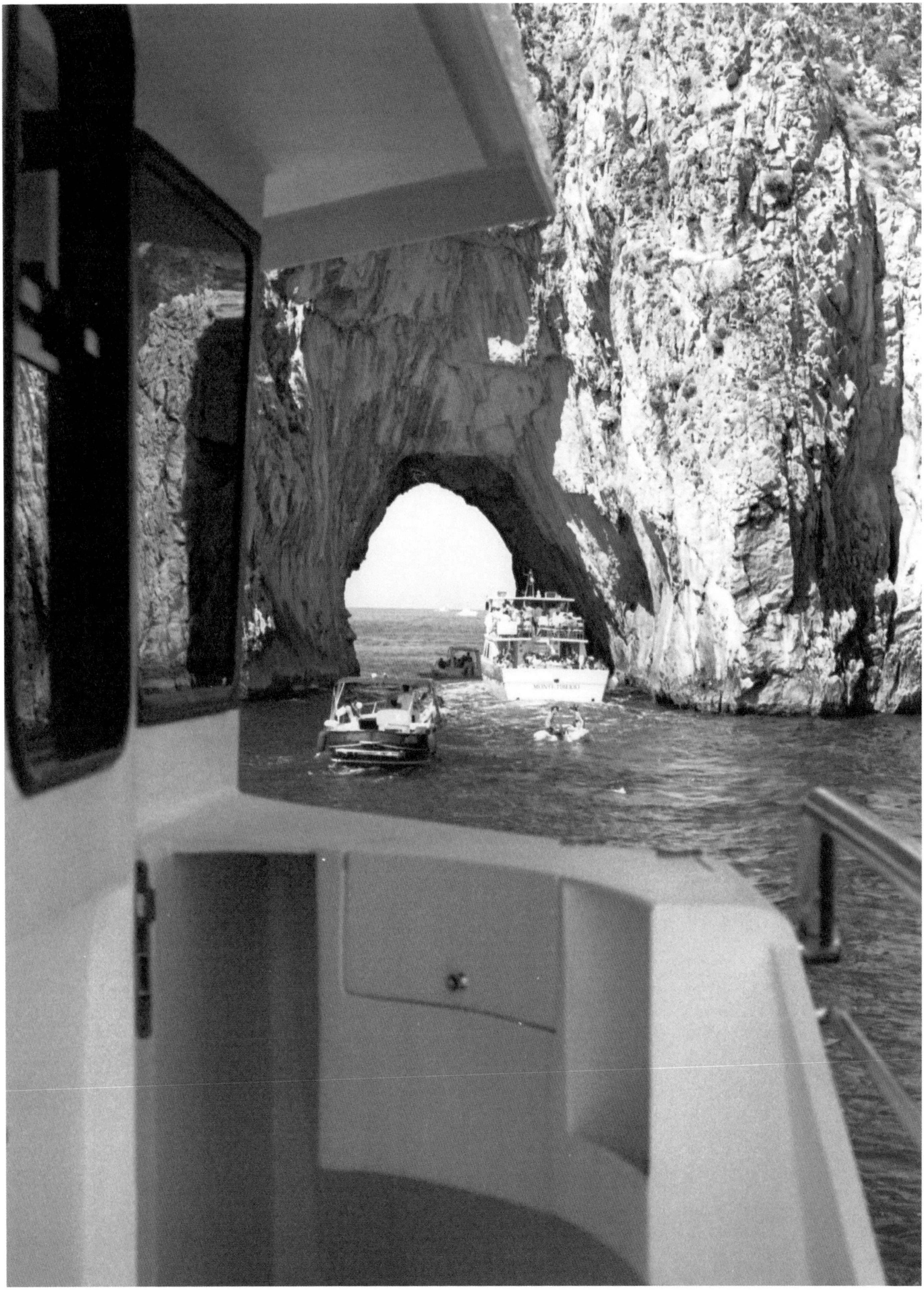

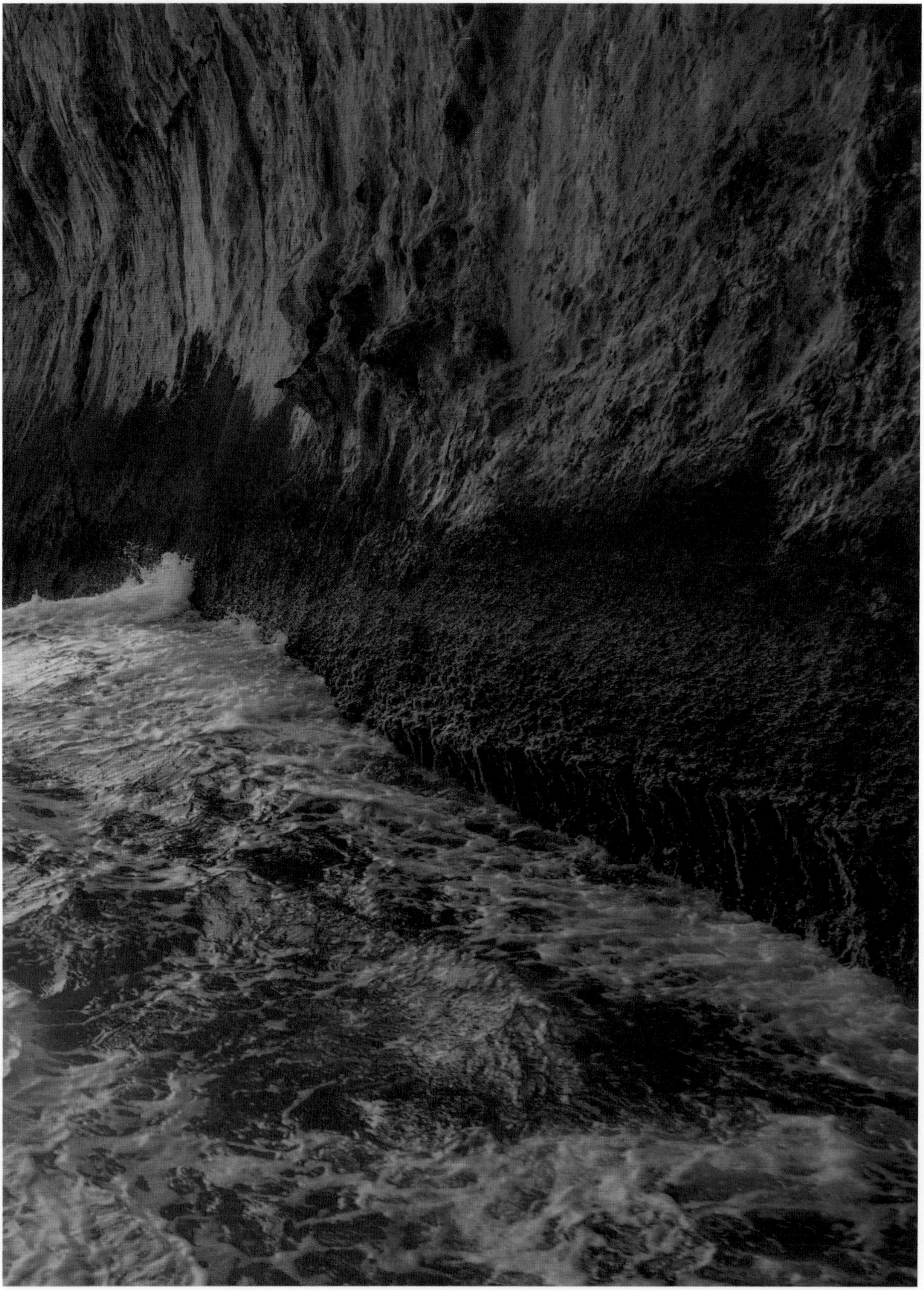

Printed in Great Britain
by Amazon

40608383R00025